"I Wouldn't Start From Here!"

A travelling supporters guide to British Rugby League grounds

By Peter Lush and Dave Farrar

LONDON LEAGUE PUBLICATIONS Ltd.

"I Wouldn't Start From Here!"

A travelling supporters guide to British Rugby League grounds

© Copyright Peter Lush and Dave Farrar

The moral right of Peter Lush and Dave Farrar to be identified as the authors has been asserted.

Photographs by Peter Lush, and may not be reproduced without permission.

A CIP catalogue record for this book is available from the British Library.

First published in Great Britain in March 1996 by:

London League Publications Ltd.
P.O. Box 10441
London E14 0SB

ISBN: 0 9526064 5 3

Design by: Stephen McCarthy Graphic Design
23, Carol Street, London NW1 0HT

Printed and bound by: Juma Printing and Publishing
44, Wellington Street, Sheffield S1 4HD

Dedicated to Harry Stammers - supporter of Fulham, London Crusaders and London Broncos since 1980, and still travelling to every game at the age of 77.

Preface

The idea for this book came when we were driving around the York ring road, in a snow storm, trying to find Ryedale Stadium to watch York play London Crusaders. This experience, added to similar ones in Leigh, Oldham, and other parts of the Rugby League world, showed us the need for this book.

One of the great strengths of Rugby League is that we have not had to include in this book advice about "safety" for away fans. Whilst local rivalry can be fierce, Rugby League usually manages to provide a welcome for away supporters. We hope this book will encourage more supporters to travel to away matches supporting their team, and to visit other clubs as well.

And for any observant "trainspotters" - yes we do know that British Rail is being privatised, but felt it was simpler to use BR to indicate a railway, as different from metro or underground station.

Peter Lush and Dave Farrar

How to use this book

We recommend using a standard road map as well as this book. The maps are not drawn to scale, and are only meant to cover the areas very close to grounds, where it is easy to get lost. The road directions are the most easy to follow routes, and sometimes try to avoid city centres, where there is more likely to be bad traffic.

We have done our best to ensure this book is accurate. However, there are bound to be mistakes in the book. We visited every ground, but there can be changes in facilities, road layout etc that we are not aware of at the time of production. Please let us know any mistakes you find, so we can make corrections in the next edition.

Please send corrections to: London League Publications Ltd, .P.O. Box 10441, London E14 0SB

Please note that the authors and London League Publications Ltd do not accept any liability for any loss, injury or inconvenience sustained by people as a result of using information or advice in this book.

Thank You

We would like to thank all the club officials, supporters club officials, tourist information centre staff and travel information phone line staff who gave us information for this book. The support and sponsorship from the Rugby League Supporters Association were also very helpful. Sandra's consistent support was very important. As well as the above, we would like to thank the following for their support:

Association of Sports Historians
John Drake
Friends of London Rugby League
Harry Edgar and *Open Rugby*
Heather Felston
Lancashire Federation RLSC
League Express
Lloyds Bank
London Broncos RLSC
London Calling! fanzine
Ian Lush
Chris McCracken
Henry Miles
Huw Richards
Glyn Robbins
Rugby Leaguer
Irvin Saxton
Yorkshire Federation RLSC

And everyone who subscribed to the book in advance

About the title

We have all had the experience of winding down the car window and asking a local "do you know the way to ...?". You can tell from the look on their face that they know where your destination is, but then a worried look appears. "Well, I wouldn't start from here" they say. This guide will hopefully avoid such situations for travelling Rugby League fans in the future - wherever they are starting from.

Foreword

Travelling to an away match is a unique experience for many Rugby League fans. Some of the greatest away trips are memorable not for what happened when two teams clashed on the pitch but for the occasion itself and the journeys to and from the game. To many the highlights of away travel are meeting new people who share a common bond, and for those who have experienced Rugby League outside Britain, sampling new cultures.

Not so long ago, however, "going away" was simply about getting from A to B as quickly as possible, usually by the M62. In the winter months those fans who were mad enough to set off often braved gale force winds and driving rain. Having arrived at a particular town, the next challenge was finding the ground. Two RLSA members once tried to use an old guide to get to Keighley. What followed was a magical mystery tour of confused routes and chaotic directions that led to the ultimate indignity of all. They missed the kick off.

During the 1995 Halifax Centenary World Cup, "going away" was given a new definition. Fans travelled from all over Britain and the world to experience international Rugby League at less familiar venues, such as Vetch Field in Swansea, Ninian Park, Cardiff, and the Gateshead International Stadium. For many travelling fans the main highlight was exploring the side routes - heading to Wembley via St. Albans or driving down the Head of the Valleys road into Swansea.

As we enter the era of Super League (or the Stones Euro League as it is officially known) and summer Rugby these memories are a prelude of what is to come. Rugby League will no longer be about just travelling to a game. Evening kick offs will mean that days will be left free.... Free to experience the sights around the grounds, to visit local tourist attractions or simply to while away the hours enjoying the local beer.

The RLSA sees the need for summer Rugby to be promoted in a way that will continue to draw in existing fans while attracting a new audience. We are therefore delighted to sponsor "I Wouldn't Start From Here", which we feel is a book which does just that. The guide contains a wealth of information. The travel information included is more than a glorified road map and provides advice for those who prefer to utilise public transport.

There is background information plus details of the facilities of each club mentioned and for those tempted by a longer stay in a particular area there are local tourist information contact numbers and addresses.

The guide embraces the whole spectrum of the Rugby League community from the Super League clubs to the BARLA National Conference and in doing so offers something for everybody. In short "I Wouldn't Start From Here" is a highly recommended addition to any Rugby League fan's bookshelf. Once purchased I feel it will be a much thumbed one too.

Heather Felston
National Chair, Rugby League Supporters Association

Travelling away - over the Pennines for a cup match

Contents

The Super League:

International grounds:

First Division:

Amateur Clubs:

Stop Press:

Useful information 99

Notes 102

Advertisements 103

Second Division:

On the way to the match - Castleford November 1995

Castleford v London Broncos November 1995

The Super League

Bradford Bulls
Castleford
Halifax
Leeds
London Broncos
Oldham Bears
Paris St Germain
Sheffield Eagles
St Helens
Warrington
Wigan
Workington Town

On television - Sky camera at Castleford

Bradford Bulls

Description of ground: One of the most famous grounds in Rugby League. Holds the attendance record for a Rugby League match at the 1954 Challenge Cup Final Replay. An ideal venue for the summer. The spaciousness lends itself to family entertainment, which will be a key feature at Bradford Bulls matches.

Ground address: Odsal Stadium, Rooley Avenue, Bradford BD6 1BS
Ground telephone No.: 01274-733899. Fax: 01274-724730
Club Call: 0891-122778
Match day information: 01274-733899
Office address: Odsal Stadium, Rooley Avenue, Bradford BD6 1BS
Office telephone No.: 01274-733899.
Ticket information phone no.: 01274-733899
Capacity: 28,000
Number of seats: 5,850
Advance ticket availability: Contact Club Office

Price reductions for:
Children: Yes
Pensioners: Yes
Unemployed: Yes
(With passport to leisure card)
Students: No
Disabled: No

Disabled supporters:
Facilities: Yes. Bars accessible to the disabled
Wheelchair access: Yes
Disabled toilets: Yes
The Blind: No special facilities

Club Shop:
Address: As above
Telephone: As above

Opening hours: Weekdays except Thursday: 9.00 am to 5.30 pm, Thursday: 9.00 am to 9.00 pm.
Match days: 3.30 pm to 6.00 pm and 7.30 pm to 8.00 pm
Mail order service: To club shop, or credit card orders by telephone

Supporters Club:
Address: Mr J. Hunt, 27, Wesley Ave, Low Moor, Bradford BD12 0NX
Telephone: 01274-679844

Food and drink:
In the ground: 4 catering kiosks, including pies, burgers & hot drinks.

Touchdown Restaurant: Advance reservations only. Special matchday package available. Contact the marketing department on 01274-733899
Bars: Trevor Foster lounge

Transport:
Car parking: Car parks at Richard Dunn sports centre (free) & Stadium car park (£1).
Public transport:
Information: 0113-245-7676
Nearest BR station: Bradford Forster Square & Metro Interchange stations, both in town centre.

Buses: From Metro Interchange: 268, 363, 622, 623, 624, 625, 626, 627, 634, 681, 682. 508 (Leeds to Halifax)

General Facilities:
Lounges can be booked for private parties, also for meetings, seminars etc. Telephone: 01274-724573

Tourist Information:
Bradford Tourist Information Office, National Museum of Photography, Film & TV, Pictureville, Bradford, West Yorkshire BD1 1NQ
Tel.: 01274-753678.

Directions by Road:
Take M62, junction 26, then M606. At end of M606, take A6036 (Rooley Avenue). Odsal stadium is on left.
From north of Bradford: Take ring road (A6177) to junction with M606, then as above.
From city centre: Follow signs for M606, then as above.

Local Map:

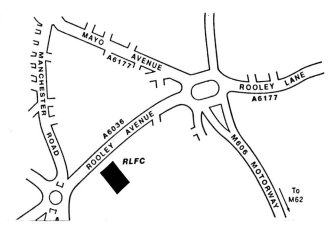

3

Castleford

Description of ground: Main stand on one side, covered terracing behind one goal and on other side. The Lock Lane ARLFC social club\ pub (The Early Bath) is also on Wheldon Road.

Ground address: Wheldon Road, Castleford, WF10 2SD
Ground telephone No.: 01977-552674
Club Call: 0891-424142
Match day information: 01977-552674
Office address: As above
Office telephone No.: As above. **Fax:** 01977-518007
Ticket information phone no.: As above
Capacity: 11,750
Number of seats: 1,500
Advance ticket availability: Sometimes

Price reductions for:
Children: Yes
Age: Under 16
Pensioners: Yes
Unemployed: No
Students: No
Disabled: Yes
(Blind or wheelchair only)

Disabled supporters:
Facilities: Free admission to wheelchair users
Wheelchair access: Enclosure on first come first served basis
Disabled toilets: No
The blind: Free admission to totally blind

Club Shop:

Location: On Wheldon Road by turnstiles
Address: As above
Telephone: 01977-553309
Opening hours: Wednesday to Saturday 9.30 am to 12 midday, and 1 hour before matches

Supporters Club:
Address: Ms D. Howard, 163, Hugh St, Castleford WF10 4DU

Food and drink:
In the ground: Restaurant open to away supporters. Kiosks.
Bars: Yes

Transport:
Car parking: Training field adjacent to Wheldon Road. Street

parking also available
Public transport: Information:
0113-245-7676
Nearest BR station: Castleford
Buses: 167,168, 468. West
Riding Buses depot is a few
minutes walk from the ground on
Wheldon Road.

Tourist Information:
Wakefield Tourist Information,
Town Hall, Wood Street,
W.Yorkshire WF1 2HQ.
Tel: 01924-295000/1,
Fax: 01924-295283.

Directions by road:
From west: M62 take junction 31, A655 to Castleford. At roundabout turn
right into A6032 (Aire Street). At next roundabout, take second exit, which
is Wheldon Road. Ground is on right.
From east: M62 take junction 32, A639 to Castleford. Turn right onto
A656, at roundabout with A6032, turn right into Wheldon Road. Ground on
right.
From north and south: Either A1, then M62 as for east above, or take
B6136 from A1, which joins A639. Turn right, then as for east above.

Local map:

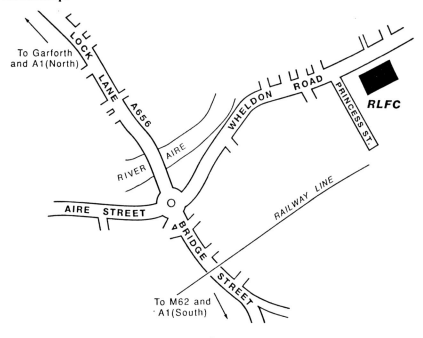

Halifax

Description of ground: In complex shared with Halifax Cricket and Bowls clubs. Pavilion in corner of ground houses club offices. Main stand on one side, covered terrace on other side, and behind one goal.

Ground address: Thrum Hall, Thrum Hall Lane, Halifax, HX1 4TL
Ground telephone No.: 01422-361026
Club Call: 0891-121577
Match day information: 01422-361026
Office address: The Pavilion, Thrum Hall, Halifax HX1 4TL
Office telephone No.: 01422-361026
Ticket information phone no.: 01422-361026
Capacity: 9,852
Number of seats: 1,219
Advance ticket availability: 14 days prior to the game

Price reductions for:
Children: Yes
Age: Up to 16
Pensioners: Yes
Unemployed: No
Students: No
Disabled: Yes

Disabled supporters:
Facilities: Hard core area behind goals
Wheelchair access: Yes
Disabled toilets: No
The blind: No special facilities

Club Shop:
Address: As above
Telephone: None
Opening hours: Thursday 7.30 pm to 9.00 pm

Match days: 1.00 pm to 3.00 pm
(Sundays) 6.00 pm to 7.30 pm
(Midweek)

Supporters Club:
Address: Mrs J. Mitchell, 48, Weatherhouse Tce, Pellon, Halifax, HX2 0PU. Tel.: 01422-366701

Food and drink:
In the ground: 3 refreshment kiosks
Bars: Taverners Bar, Cricket Club

Transport:
Car parking: None. Some street parking.
Public transport:
Information: 0113-245-7676
Nearest BR station: Halifax

Buses: 520, 522 and 535 from town centre

Halifax Tourist Information Office, Piece Hall, Halifax, W.Yorskhire, HX1 1RE. Tel: 01422-354264

Tourist Information:

Directions by Road:

From east, west and south: M62 take junction 24, A629 signposted Halifax. Stay on A629 into town centre, through Cow Green, and fork left into Pellon Lane. Fork left into Hanson Lane, and left into Thrum Hall Lane. Ground is on right.

Local Map:

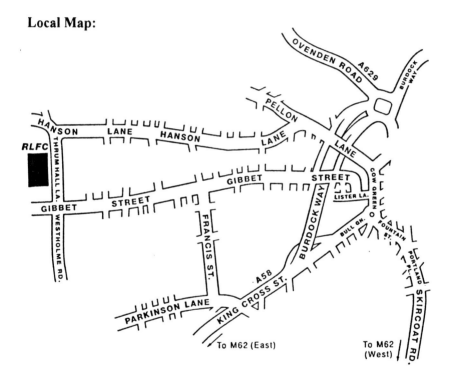

Leeds

Description of ground: Part of complex with Yorkshire county cricket ground. Large main stand (joint stand with cricket ground) and covered terrace, terracing behind both goals uncovered. Club have major development plans.

Ground address: Headingley, St. Michaels Lane, Leeds LS6 3BR
Ground telephone No.: 0113-2786181 Fax: 0113-2754284
Club Call: 0891-555888
Match day information: As above
Office address: As above
Office telephone No.: As above
Ticket information phone no.: As above
Capacity: 27,500
Number of seats: 5,713
Advance ticket availability: Contact club as above

Price reductions for:
Children: Yes
Age: Under 16
Pensioners: Yes
Unemployed: No
Students: No
Disabled: Yes

Club Shop:
Address: As above
Telephone: As above
Opening hours: Week days 9.00am to 7.00pm. Saturday 9.00 to 12 noon.
Match days: 10.00 to 5.15 pm

Disabled supporters:
Facilities: Area for 25 wheelchairs. Parking (on season ticket basis)
Wheelchair access: Viewing area. Bars accessible
Disabled toilets: Yes
The blind: 12 seats wired to pick up match commentary. Headphones provided.

Supporters Club:
Address: Mrs A. Wood, 46, New Adel Lane, Adel, Leeds LS16 6AN
Telephone: 0113-261-1656

Food and drink:
In the ground: Kiosks - hot and cold food
Bars: South stand and Len Hutton Bar Main stand. Supporters Social Club, South Stand Car Park

8

Transport:

Car parking: Limited parking within ground. Street parking available.

Public transport:
Information: 0113-245-7676
Nearest BR station: Headingley.
Information: 0113-244-8133
Buses: 56 & 57 from city centre bus station. 74,76 & 77 from Infirmary Street

General Facilities:

Conference and banqueting facilities within pavilion. Parties from 25 to 250. On match days: Radio Headingley on 1413 AM.

Tourist Information:

Regional Travel Centre, The Arcade, City Station, Leeds, W.Yorkshire, LS1 1PL.
Tel.: 0113-2478301/2.
Fax: 0113-2478036

Directions by Road:

From south, east: M1 junction 47, then M621 junction 2 A643 towards city centre. Join A58(M) and follow signs for A660 (Otley, Skipton). Join A660, which becomes Headingley Lane. Turn left into Kirkstall Lane North, and ground is on left.
From west: M62 junction 27 take M621 to junction 2, then as above.

Local Map:

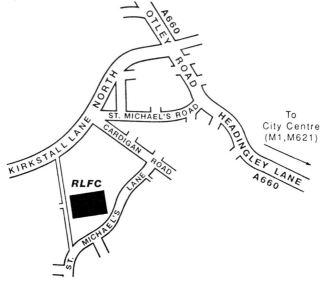

London Broncos

Descrption of ground: Modernised football stadium. All seater - good views from both sides.

Ground address: Charlton Athletic FC, The Valley, Floyd Road, London SE7 8BL
Ground telephone No.: 0181-293-4567 (matchdays)
Club Call No: 0839-333034
Match day information: 0181-293-4567
Office address: As above
Office telephone No.: 0181-776-6670 Fax: 0181-776-6533
Ticket Information Phone No.: 0181-776-6670
Capacity: 15,000
Number of seats: 15,000
Advance ticket availability:

Price reductions for:
Children: Yes
Age: Under 12 free
Pensioners: Yes
Unemployed: Yes
Students: Yes
Disabled: Yes

Disabled supporters:

Facilities:
Wheelchair access: Yes
Disabled toilets: Yes
The blind: No special facilities

Club Shop:

Address: As above
Telephone: As above
Opening hours: Match days

Match days: See above

Supporters Club:
Contact: Barry and Gwen Warren
Telephone: 01322-528504

Food and drink:
In the ground: Snack bars
Bars: Yes

Transport:

Car parking: Street parking and car parks near ground
Public transport:
Information: 0171-222-1234
Nearest BR station: Charlton
0171-928-5100
Buses: 177, 180.

General Facilities: Function room for hire

Tourist Information: London Tourist Board, 26, Grosvenor Gardens, SW1W 01DU.

Accommodation: 0171-824-8844 Greenwich Tourist Information, 46, Greenwich Church Street, Greenwich, SE10 9BL. Tel: 0181-858-6376

Directions by Road:

From north: Take A1, then M11 towards London. At end of motorway, junction 4, stay in left hand lane. Take North Circular Road (A406) signposted London (East) and City, and stay on A406. Ignore signs for A12 & Blackwall Tunnel. At end of A406, turn right at roundabout onto A13. Go over Canning Town flyover, and after traffic lights, get into left hand lane to turn into Blackwall Tunnel (A102). Turn left into tunnel, and stay in left hand lane. Take second exit, A206, left. Pass trading estate on left, and ground is on right hand side behind houses. Some parking on this road, but there are restrictions on street parking. (This is not the shortest route, but the easiest for drivers not familiar with London. The Blackwall tunnel can be busy, so allow an hour from the end of the M11).

Local Map:

Oldham Bears

Description of ground: Main stand largely not used. Covered terracing behind one goal, seating and terracing behind other. Oldham are planning to move within two years to a new stadium.

Ground address: The Pavilion, Watersheddings, Oldham OL4 2PB
Ground telephone No.: 0161-624-4865 or 0161-652-5244.
Club Call: 0891-440070
Match day information: As above
Office address: As above
Office telephone No.: As above. Fax: 0161-624-1003
Ticket information phone no.: As above
Capacity: 9,315
Number of seats: 685 (some not in use)
Advance ticket availability: Contact Club Office

Price reductions for:
Children: Yes
Age: School age
Pensioners: Yes
Unemployed: No
Students: No
Disabled: No

Disabled supporters:
Facilities: Limited disabled viewing area on application. Special car park. To use car park, phone 0161-624-4865 prior to matchday to reserve place.
Wheelchair access: Yes. Social Club bar accessible to disabled supporters.
Disabled toilets: No
The Blind: No special facilities

Club Shop: The Pavilion. By main stand entrance. Also shop at Town Square Shopping centre.
Opening hours: 9.00am - 5.00pm weekdays, Sat: 9.30 - 11.30am.
Town Square: 9.00 am to 5.00 pm Monday to Saturday
Match days: At ground: 12.30 pm to 5.00 pm

Supporters Club:
Address: Ms A.Collinge, 55, Littlemoor La, Oldham OL4 2RR
Tel: 0161-633-6780

Food and drink:
Social club open to any supporters
In ground: Kiosks, sweets, pies etc. *Bars:* Members bar in Pavilion

Transport:

Car parking: Some at ground, also side streets.
Public transport: Information: 0161-228-7811
Nearest BR station: Oldham Mumps
Buses: 82, 83.

Tourist Information:

Oldham Tourist Information, Central Library, Union Street, Oldham Lancs OL1 1DN.
Tel: 0161-627-1024.
Fax: 0161-627-1025.

Directions by Road:

From east or west: Take M62 to junction 22, take A672 signposted Saddleworth. This becomes Ripponden Road, and ground is on left, off Herbert Street. Side street parking off Ripponden Road.
From south and Manchester: Take A62 from central Manchester. Pass Oldham Mumps station on right. A62 becomes Huddersfield Road, and Ripponden Road forks off to left. (N.B. From south it may be quicker to avoid Manchester, and use M62).
N.B. At least 6 games in 1996 season will be played at Oldham Athletic FC's Boundary Park. The ground is near the junction of the A627(M) with the A663, and is off the A627, which runs from this junction. **Check press for venue of games.**

Local Map:

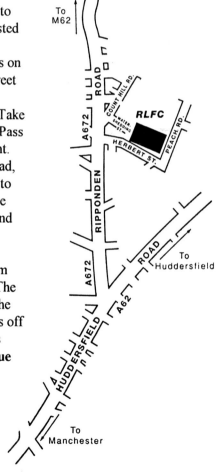

Paris St Germain

Ground address: Stade (Stadium) Sebastein Charlety, 79, Boulevard Kellerman, 13th District, Paris

Ground telephone No.: (00-331-) 44166000 (dialling from Britain).
Capacity: 20,000
Number of seats: 20,000

Disabled supporters:
Facilities:
Wheelchair access:
Disabled toilets:
The Blind:

Food and drink:
In the ground:
Bars:

Transport:

From Britain:
Eurostar trains: 3 hours from Waterloo to Paris Gare du Nord. Information: 0345-881881.
Flights: British Airways, Air France and British Midland.
Coach: National Express. Daily buses from London. Telephone: 0990-808080
Cars: Shuttle Folkestone - Calais: Information: 0990-353535

In Paris:
Car parking: Car parks at Rue Thomire and Avenue Pierre de Courbetin
Public transport:
Nearest RER station: Cite Universitaire on line B2 or B4. (Blue line on maps). Runs from Gare du Nord main line station. Buses: PC. 21, 28, 38 and 67 run near the Stadium.
Transport: Information:
Buses: (00-331-) 43461414.
Trains: (00-331-) 45656000
Paris Visite travel passes available for 3 or 5 days.

Tourist Information:
Office du Tourisme et des Congres de Paris-Accueil de France, 127 avenue Champes Elysees, 8th District. Tel: 00-331-49525354
British Embassy: 42669142
To telephone Britain, dial 19,44 then area code and number.

Road directions:
From M62: Take M6, then M1, or M1 or A1 to M25 London Orbital Motorway. Head east, cross Dartford River crossing, and take junction 2 (A2) for Dover, or take junction 3 (M20) for Folkestone and Channel Tunnel.

From Calais: A16 motorway, follow signs for Paris and turn onto A26 motorway. Pass signs for Arras and turn right onto A1 to Paris. Turn left onto ring road, and take turn off for Porte de Gentilly - Avenue Pierre de Coubertin. Turn right into Boulevard Kellerman, and stadium is on right. **(Check that your insurance covers you for driving in France)**

N.B.We understand that the Paris v Wigan match in the 1996 season will not be played at this stadium. Check with clubs or Rugby League for further information about venue.

Local map:

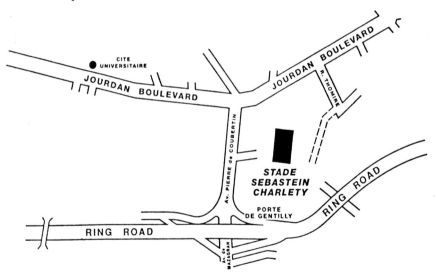

15

Sheffield Eagles

Description of ground: Modern athletics stadium. Only main stand used for Rugby League matches. Good facilities, but can lack atmosphere because of large areas of empty seats.

Ground address: Don Valley Stadium, Worksop Road, Sheffield, S9 3TL
Ground telephone No.: 0114-256-0607
(Monday to Friday 9.00 am to 5.00 pm)
Match day information: 0114-261-7966 (from noon onwards)
Office address: 824, Attercliffe Road, Sheffield S9 3RS
Office telephone No.: 0114-261-0326. **Fax:** 0114-261-0303
Club Call: None
Ticket information phone no.: 0114-261-0326
Capacity: 25,000
Number of seats: 25,000
Advance ticket availability: No

Price reductions for:
Children: Yes
Age: Up to 16
Pensioners: Yes
Unemployed: No
Students: Yes
Disabled: Yes

Disabled supporters:
Facilities: viewing area.
Wheelchair access: Yes
Disabled toilets: Yes
The blind: Yes

Club Shop:
Address: Orchard Square, Fargate, Sheffield
Telephone: 0114-261-0326
Opening hours: 9.30am - 4.30pm

Match days: One and half hours before kick off and half hour after (at ground)

Supporters Club:
Address: None

Food and drink:
In the ground: Catering units on concourse
Bars: None

Transport:
Car parking: £1 - Attercliffe or Coleridge Road
Public transport:
Nearest BR station: Sheffield Midland (main line). Local trains to Attercliffe or Meadowhall.

Buses:From Sheffield interchange No.130. Supertram service. Information 01709-515151.

General Facilities: Creche from 18 months upwards. £1 includes drink & snack. Stadium has many other sports facilities.

Tourist Information: Sheffield Tourist Information Centre, Peace Gardens, Sheffield, S1 2HH. Tel.: 0114-273-4671/2. Fax: 0114-272-4225.

Directions by road:
From south: M1 junction 34, take A6178 into Sheffield. Stadium is on left.
From east, west and north: M1 junction 34, take A6109 into Sheffield. Turn left into A6021 (Hawke St) and right onto A6178 (Attercliffe Common), and stadium is on left. N.B. Junction 34 is used for the Meadowhall shopping centre, and therefore can be very busy.
Sheffield are planning to play 3 games at Sheffield United's Bramall Lane ground in 1996. Bramall Lane (A621) is off the A61 to Chesterfield. Use M1 junction 33, A57 towards city centre, then A61.

Local Map:

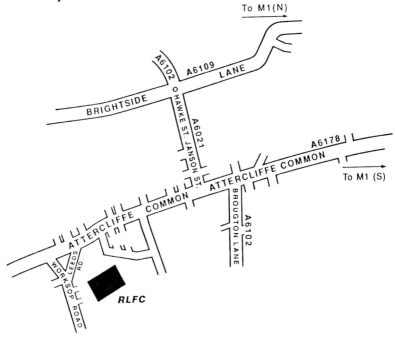

17

St Helens

Description of ground: Large main stand, covered terracing on other side and behind one goal. One of the better grounds in Rugby League, but in need of a modernisation programme to provide more seats and cover.

Ground address: Knowsley Road, St Helens, Merseyside WA10 4AD
Ground telephone No.: 01744-23697 or 01839-664422
Club Call: 0839-664422
Match day information: As above
Office address: As above
Office telephone No.: As above. Fax: 01744-451302
Ticket information phone no.: As above
Capacity: 17,300
Number of seats: 2,270
Advance ticket availability: Yes for stand admission

Price reductions for:
Children: Yes
Age: Under 16
Pensioners: Yes
Unemployed: No
Students: No
Disabled: Yes. Supporters in wheelchairs admitted free

Disabled supporters:
Facilities: Viewing area. Bars accessible.
Wheelchair access: Yes
Disabled toilets: Yes
The blind: Scheme being investigated to set up segregated area in the main stand for the blind including commentary on match.

Club Shop:
Address: As above.
Telephone: 01744-58269
Opening hours: 9.30am- 5.00pm weekdays and on training nights
Match days: Yes

Supporters Club:
Address: Mr J.Powell, 1, Houghtons Lane, Eccleston, St Helens
Tel: 0151-426-8686

Food and drink:
In the ground: Mobile kiosks.
Bars: Cabaret Bar open to visitors. Supporters club card admits for free admission

18

Transport:
Car parking: Small car park £1
Public transport: Information:
Mersey Travel 0151-236-7676
Nearest BR station: Thatto Heath
(1 mile)
Buses: 121 and 122 from town
centre

Tourist Information:
Liverpool Tourist Information,
Merseyside Welcome Centre,
Clayton Square, Shopping Centre,
Liverpool, Merseyside, L1 1QR.
Tel.: 0151-709-3631.

Directions by Road:
From east, west and south: M62 take junction 7, then A570 to town centre.
At roundabout, turn left onto A58 (Westfield Street). Turn right into
Dunriding Lane, at end of road turn left into Knowsley Road, ground is on
left.
From north: M6 take junction 24, A58, then turn right onto A580. Take
A570 towards town centre, then turn right onto A58, then as above.

Local Map:

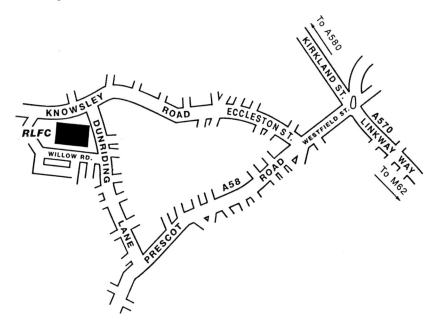

Warrington

Description of ground: Large main stand, covered terracing behind both goals. Limited terracing on other side.

Ground address: Wilderspool Stadium, Wilderspool Causeway, Warrington WA4 6PY
Ground telephone No.: 01925-635338 or 01925-634903
Club Call: 0891-888645
Match day information: As Above
Office address: As above
Office telephone No.: As above. **Fax:** 01925-571744
Ticket information phone no.: 01925-635338 or 01925-634903
Capacity: 11,140
Number of seats: 2,013
Advance ticket availability: Yes - two matches in advance. On match days from 11.00 am (for 3 pm kick off)

Price reductions for:
Children: Yes
Age: Under 16
Pensioners: Yes
Unemployed: No
Students: Yes
(Season tickets only)
Disabled: Yes

Disabled supporters:
Facilities: Viewing Area - west terrace
Wheelchair access: Yes (door 26)
Disabled toilets: Yes
The blind: No special facilities - but will accommodate on request

Club Shop:
Address: Market Stall, Warrington Market. Also shop in Birchwood shopping mall
Telephone: 01925-635338
Opening hours: Mon-Sat 9.00am-5.00pm
Match days: Souveniers on sale at lottery office from 1.00 pm and from kiosk on western terrace.

Supporters Club:
Address: Mr S. Lewandowski, 41, Ryedale Avenue, Warrington.
Tel.: 01925-633806

Food and drink:
In the ground: Three snack bars on terraces and two in main stand.
Bars: Not open to visitors - members only

Transport:
Car parking: Pay car park adjacent to ground. Free car parks (signposted) within three minutes walk of ground.
Public transport: Information: 0151-236-7676
Nearest BR station: Warrington Bank Quay (Main London - Glasgow line), Warrington Central (Manchester - Liverpool line). Both 10 minute walk from ground.
Buses: 5, 5a, 6 and 6a from Golden Square Bus station

Tourist Information:
Warrington Tourist Information Centre, 21, Rylands Street, Warrington, Cheshire, WA1 1EJ.
Tel.: 01985--218548.
Fax: 01985-846154.

Directions by Road:
From north, east or west: M62 to junction 9, then A49 signposted Warrington. Stay on A49, which becomes Wilderspool Causeway, and ground is on left.
From south: M6 junction 20, take M56 west. At junction 10 take A49 signposted Warrington. This becomes Wilderspool Causeway, and ground is on right.

Local Map:

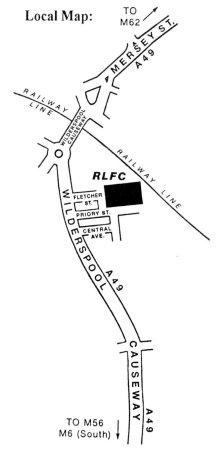

21

Wigan

Description of ground: Largest club ground in Britain. Stands on both sides with terracing in front, new stand behind one goal, and covered terracing behind other. Regular venue for international matches.

Ground address: Central Park, Wigan, Greater Manchester WN1 1XF
Ground telephone No.: 01942-231321
Club Call: 0891-121158
Match day information: 01942-231321
Office address: As above
Office telephone No.: 01942-231321 **Fax:** 01942-820111
Ticket information phone no.:01942-231321
Capacity: 30,000
Number of seats: 5,302
Advance ticket availability: By credit card on 01942-231321, usually 10 days prior to a game

Price reductions for:
Children: Yes
Age: Up to 16
Pensioners: Yes
Unemployed: No
Students: No
Disabled: Yes
(Wheelchair users)

Disabled supporters:

Facilities: Viewing area. Bars accessible
Wheelchair access: In front of Whitbread stand
Disabled toilets: Yes
The blind: Live commentrary given from hospital commentary box

Club Shop:
Address: Central Park, Wigan, WN1 1XF. Also in Marketgate shopping centre
Telephone:
01942-246531(Central Park)
01942-821484 (Marketgate)
 01942-246531 (Mail order)
Opening hours: 9.00am-5.00pm (Monday -Friday)
Match days: 12.00 midday - 3.00pm and half hour afterwards

Supporters Club:
Address: Ms A. Dempsey , 19, Guildford Cres, Beech Hill,Wigan
Telephone number:
01942-246371

Food and drink:
In the ground: Mobile food vans
open during games
Bars: Douglas and Sullivan Bars
open to visitors

Transport:
Car parking: Colinfield car park -
cost £1.00. Also limited street
parking.
Public transport: Information:
0161-228-7811.
Nearest BR station: Wigan
Wallgate and Wigan North
Western - both 15 minutes walk

Directions by Road:
From east: M62, take junction 14-
M61 north. Take junction 6, and turn
left onto A6going south. Immediately
turn right into Dicconson Lane
(B5239). Turn left onto Wigan Road
(B5238) and follow this road into town
centre. Central park is on the right,
down Greenough Street. Parking is
very restricted in the town centre and
around the ground.
From west: Take A580, turn left onto
A49, and just beyond town centre, this
becomes Central Park Way and ground
is on left.
From north: M6 take junction 27,
A5209, signposted Wigan. Join A49
then as above for west.
From south: M6 take junction 25,
A49, signposted Wigan, then as above
for west.

Buses: Wigan Bus depot - 15
minutes walk. 342, 352, 362, 372,
639, 640, 654, 664,674 all run by
ground.

General Facilities: Riverside
Club at ground

Tourist Information:
Wigan Tourist Information Office,
Trencherfield Mill, Wallgate,
Lancashire, WN3 4EL.
Tel: 01942-825677.
Fax: 01942-828540.

Local Map:

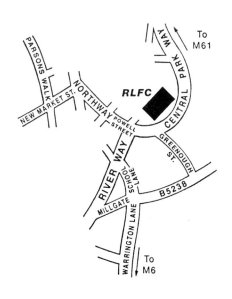

Workington Town

Description of ground: Main stand and enclosure on one side, covered terrace on other. New stands behind both goals being built for new season. Former speedway stadium.

Ground address: Derwent Park, Bridge Street, Workington, CA14 2HG
Ground telephone No.: 01900-603609.
Club Call: 0891-884448
Match day information: 01900-603609
Office address: As above
Office telephone No.: As above. **Fax:** 01900-871103
Ticket information phone no.: As above
Capacity: 10,000
Number of seats: 4,800 (1,200 in grandstand)
Advance ticket availability: Grandstand only

Price reductions for:
Children: Yes:
Age: Under 16
Pensioners: Yes
Unemployed: No
Students: No
Disabled: Yes

Disabled supporters:
Facilities: Viewing area. Bars accessible
Wheelchair access: Yes
Disabled toilets: Yes
The blind: No special facilities

Club Shop:
Address: c/o Club
Match days: Kiosk at ground

Supporters Club:
Address: Gus Risman Bar, Derwent Park, Workington, CA14 2HG

Food and drink:
In the ground: Kiosks
Bars: Derwent Lounge, Gus Risman bar, Riverside bar, Presidents Bar

Transport:
Car parking: 50p beside ground
Public transport:
Nearest BR station: Workington. (3 minutes walk from ground. Limited Sunday service. Buses: To town centre. Bus station 10 minutes walk from ground. 30, 48, 300 all run near ground.

Tourist Information:
Workington Tourist Information
Office, Central Car Park,

Washington Street, Workington,
Cumbria, CA14 3AW.
Tel.: 01900-602923

Directions by Road:
M6 take junction 40, A66 signposted Keswick. After passing Keswick and Cockermouth, enter Workington. Turn right onto A596 (Bridge Street), and then right onto A597, New Bridge Road,(signposted Town Centre), pass Workington Football Club on left, go straight over roundabout, and ground is on right. Follow one way system, pass station and entrance is on left. N.B. The A66 may be very busy during the summer.

Local Map:

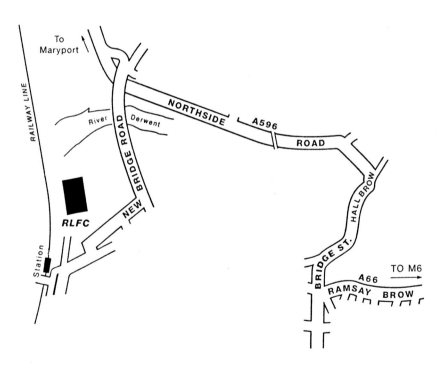

Rugby League's biggest stadium : Bradford Bulls' Odsal

The pavilion at Halifax's Thrum Hall

England v South Africa - at Rugby League

Enjoying the game - Sheffield v London Broncos - at Don Valley

27

Waiting for the World Cup - early arrivals for New Zealand v Tonga at Warrington

Central Park - home of the champions

The First Division

Batley
Dewsbury
Featherstone Rovers
Huddersfield
Hull
Keighley Cougars
Rochdale Hornets
Salford Reds
Wakefield Trinity
Whitehaven Warriors
Widnes
York

The score at Leigh - and advertising a local delicacy

Batley

Description of ground: One of the biggest slopes in Rugby League. Small stand on one side, new covered terrace at one end. Part of Mount Pleasant sports complex, including cricket and bowls clubs.

Ground address: The Pavilion, Mount Pleasant, Batley
Ground telephone No.: 01924-472208
Club Call: None
Match day information: 01924-473978 or 01924-472208
Office address: Batley RLFC, Heritage Road, Mount Pleasant, Batley, W.Yorks WF17 7NZ
Office telephone No.: 01924-470062
Ticket information phone no.: 01924-470062
Capacity: 6,000
Number of seats: 800
Advance ticket availability: When applicable

Price reductions for:
Children: Yes
Age: Under 16
Pensioners: Yes
Unemployed: Yes
Students: Yes
Disabled: No

Disabled supporters:
Facilities: Yes
Wheelchair access: Yes
Disabled toilets: Yes
The Blind: No special facilities

Club Shop:
Location: The Taverners Club
Address: As above
Telephone: 01924-470062
or 0113 2854728

Opening hours:
Weekends: 12 midday to 2.00 pm.
 Daily:7.00 pm to 11.00 pm

Supporters Club:
Address: Mr F.Galloway, 58, Woodkirk Gdns, Leeds Rd, Dewsbury WF12 7JA
Telephone Number: 01924-472895

Food and drink:
In the ground: Yes - vendors vans
Bars: In the Taverners Club

Transport:
Car parking: Yes - at the ground, and in side streets
Public transport:
Information: 0113-245-7676

Nearest BR. station: Batley. 1 mile from ground. (Trains from Huddersfield & Leeds)
Buses: 251, 252

Tourist information:
Huddersfield Tourist Information Centre, 3-5 Albion Street, W.Yorkshire, HD1 2NW
Tel: 01484-430808
Fax: 01484-451798

Directions by road:
From west: Take junction 25 on M62. Take A644 signposted Brighouse, then left onto A62 (Leeds), then turn right onto A644. Take A644 to Dewsbury, follow signs on ring road for Bradford A652. Take A652 to Batley, turn left into Taylor Street. Turn left at top of road for Mount Pleasant complex.
From east: Take junction 27 on M62. Take A62 signposted Huddersfield. Turn left onto A652, then right into Taylor Street, then as above.
From south: Take junction 40 on M1, A638 to Dewsbury, then as above from west when in Dewsbury.

Local map:

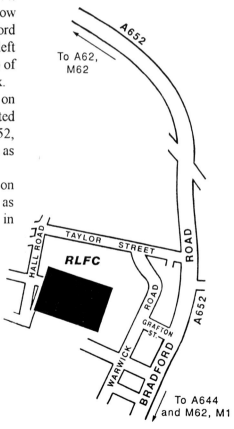

31

Dewsbury

Description of ground: New stadium after sale of previous ground. Modern main stand one one side, covered terracing on the other, nothing behind goals.

Ground address: Crown Flatt Stadium, Owl Lane, Dewsbury, W.Yorks, WF12 7JZ
Ground telephone No.: 01924-465489 (5 lines)
Club Call: The Dewsline 0891-664496
Match day information: 01924-465489 or 0891-664496
Office address: As above
Office telephone No.: As above. Fax: 01924-437201
Ticket information phone no.: As above
Capacity: 4,500 (to be increased)
Number of seats: 1,200
Advance ticket availability: When needed

Price reductions for:
Children: Yes
Age: Under 16
Pensioners: Yes
Unemployed: No
Students: No
Disabled: Yes

Disabled supporters:
Facilities: 3 designated areas. Booking for carriages.
Wheelchair access: Ramp outside stand, lift inside main stand
Disabled toilets: 3 (2 in main stand, 1 in south stand)
The blind: None as yet, can share area with radio commentators

Club Shop:
Address: As above

Telephone: As above
Opening hours: 10.00 am to 4.00 pm, Monday to Friday and on request. Matchdays from 11.30 am

Supporters Club: Red, Amber and Black Travel Club - Independent Supporters Club
Address: Kevin Whitaker, c/o Dewsbury RLFC

Food and drink:
In the ground: Lunch bookings, hot food van
Bars: Public bar, 3 bars available, 1 inside ground

Transport:
Car parking: £1. Ample parking at stadium, also street parking.

Public transport: Information: 0113-245-7676
Nearest BR station: Dewsbury
Buses: 201 (hourly on Sundays), 202 (not Sundays), 211 (not Sundays) From Bus station.

Tourist Information:
Huddersfield Tourist Information Office, 3-5 Albion Street, W.Yorkshire, HD1 2NW.
Tel: 01484-430808.
Fax: 01484-451798

Directions by Road:

From north, east or west: M62 junction 28. Take A653 signposted Dewsbury. Turn left into Owl Lane, left at roundabout, and ground is on right.
From south: M1 junction 40. Take A638 signposted Dewsbury. At roundabout turn right into Owl Lane, ground is on left.

Local Map:

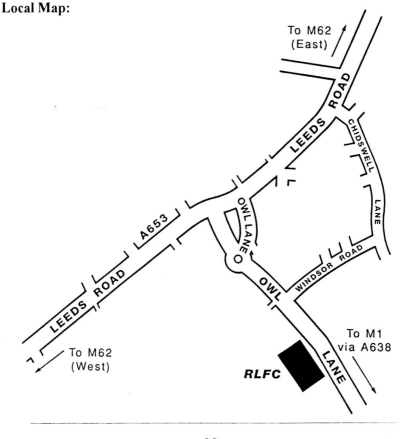

Featherstone Rovers

Description of ground: Modern stand on one side. Some covered terracing on other side, open terracing behind goals. Club shop is at side of main stand. Very close to station in town centre.

Ground address: Post Office Road, Featherstone, Pontefract, W.Yorks WF7 5EN
Ground telephone No.: 01977-602723
Club Call: 0839-333077
Match day information: 01977-602723
Office address: Post Office Road, Featherstone, Pontefract, W.Yorks WF7 5EN
Office telephone No.: 01977-602723
Ticket information phone no.: 01977-602723
Capacity: 6,680
Number of seats: 1,000
Advance ticket availability: From Football Secretary

Price reductions for:
Children: Yes
Age: Up to 16
Pensioners: Yes
Unemployed: No
Students: Yes
Disabled: Free entry to disabled area with one helper.

Disabled supporters:
Wheelchair access: Yes
Disabled toilets: Yes
The blind: No special facilities

Club Shop:
Address: c/o Club
Match days: Shop at ground
Telephone: 01977-702386

Opening hours: 9.00 am to 4.30 pm on weekdays. 9.00 am to 12.30 pm Saturdays.

Supporters Club:
Address: J. Smith (Secretary), 4, Oakland Road, Sandal, Wakefield. Telephone number: 01924-255203

Food and drink:
In the ground: Snack bars - tea & coffee, burgers etc.
Bars: In clubhouse

Transport:
Car parking: Yes - by ground. Also in side streets.

Public transport:
Information: 0113-245-7676
Nearest BR station: Featherstone.
(No Sunday service). Nearest main
line station - Wakefield Westgate.
Information: 0113-244-8133
Buses: Local services from
Pontefract, Wakefield & Castleford.
Numbers: 148,150, 146,176, 177,
178, 179, 180,181, 183, 546. Many
do not run on Sundays.

Tourist information:
Wakefield Tourist Information,
Town Hall, Wood Street, Wakefield,
W. Yorkshire, WF1 2HQ.
Tel.: 01924-295000/1
Fax: 01924-295283

Directions by Road:
M62 take junction 32, A639 to
Pontefract. Pass race course, and
turn right onto B6134. Turn left onto
B6421, follow road towards town
centre, cross railway, and Post
Office Road is on right.
Coming from Wakefield, take A645,
and turn left onto B6421. Ground is
then on right just before railway and
station.

Local Map:

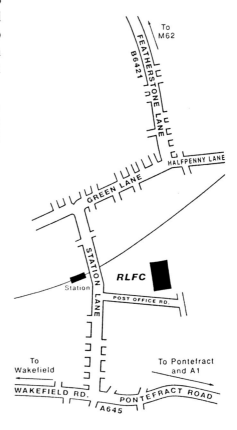

35

Huddersfield

Description of ground: Modern stadium shared with Huddersfield Town Football Club. The stand roofs make this one of the most architecturally pleasing modern stadiums in Britain. Fully seated, with plans to build fourth stand behind one goal. Very good facilities. Club shop by main entrance. Known locally as the "Big Mac".

Ground address: Alfred McAlpine Stadium, Leeds Road, Huddersfield, W.Yorkshire HD1 6PZ
Ground telephone No.: 01484-530710
Club Call: 0891-122771 or 0891-121533
Match day information: As above
Office address: As above
Office telephone No.: 01484-530710. **Fax:** 01484-531712
Ticket information phone no.: As above
Capacity: 20,000
Number of seats: 20,000
Advance ticket availability: For every match

Price reductions for:
Children: Yes
Age: Under 11 - free.
Under 15 half price
Pensioners: Yes
Unemployed: Yes
Students: Yes
Disabled: Yes

Disabled supporters:
Facilities: Half price for disabled, half price for helpers. Space for 92 wheelchairs and helpers.
Wheelchair access: Yes
Disabled toilets: Yes
The blind: Earphones available for certain reserved seats. Linked to commentary from club TV station.

Club Shop:
Address: As above
Telephone: 01484-534867
Opening hours: 9.00 am to 5.00 pm Monday to Friday.
Match days: 9.00 am to 3.00 pm Huddersfield Town FC match days. Rugby League matches: Open two hours before kick off.

Supporters Club:
Address: Mrs M.Pickard, 1,Woodbine Rd, Huddersfield HD1 6EU.
Telephone: 01484-539659

Food and drink:
In the ground: 12.00 middays - 3.00pm and then again after 5.00pm. Refreshment bars throughout the stadium.
Bars: As above.

Transport:
Car parking: £1. Two car parks at ground. Also some street parking.
Public transport: Information: 0113-245-7676
Nearest BR. station: Huddersfield.
Buses: 210,202,203 and 207 along Leeds Road. Special buses on match days from Town Centre - Byram Street - to stadium, every 10 minutes from 1 hour before kick off.

General Information:
"Lunch 'N' Crunch" - special lunch facility on match days. Contact the Club on 01484-530710.

Tourist information:
Huddersfield Tourist Information, 3-5 Albion Street, Huddersfield, W.Yorkshire, HD1 2NW.
Tel: 01484-430808.
Fax: 01484-451798.

Directions by Road:
From west: M62 take junction 25, take A644 towards Dewsbury, and turn right onto A62. Stay on A62 into Huddersfield, and stadium is on left.
From east: M62 take junction 24, A629 to Huddersfield. Turn left on ring road, and then left onto A62. Stadium is on right.
From south: M1 take junction 38, A637 to Huddersfield. Left onto A642, turn right on ring road, and right onto A62. Stadium on right.

Local Map:

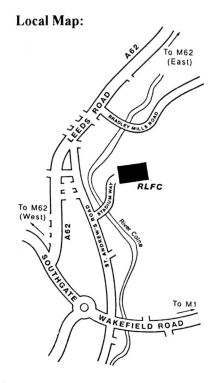

Hull

Description of ground: Main stand along one side, Threepenny Stand (seats and terracing) on other. Open terracing behind both goals. Former speedway stadium, so terracing is not close to pitch.

Ground address: The Boulevard Stadium, Airlie Street, Hull HU3 3JD
Ground telephone No.: 01482-329040
Club Call: None
Match day information: 01482-329040
Office address: As above
Office telephone No.: As above. **Fax:** 01482-320338
Ticket information phone no.: As above
Capacity: 13,200
Number of seats: 2,288
Advance ticket availability: For seats and ground

Price reductions for:
Children: Yes
Age: Under 16
Pensioners: Yes
Unemployed: No
Students: No
Disabled: No

Disabled supporters:
Facilities: Wheelchair viewing around perimeter
Wheelchair access: Yes
Disabled toilets: Yes
The blind: No special facilities

Club Shop:
Address: As above
Telephone: As above
Opening hours: Contact General Office in office hours on weekdays.

Match days: 1.30 pm until after match

Supporters Club:
Address: Mr P.Gasparelli, 2, Marsh St, Rothwell, Leeds LS26 0AE
Telephone number: 01482-2829020

Food and drink:
In the ground: Leagues club bar inside ground. Also kiosks.
Bars: Social club outside ground

Transport:
Car parking: None. Street parking nearby.
Public transport:
Nearest BR station: Hull Paragon
Buses: Hull Corporation 1 & 2 from Central Bus station.

EYMS: 60,64,66,151,155,181 from Central Bus station.

Tourist Information:
City Information Service, Central Library, Albion Street, Hull, Humberside, HU1 3TF.
Tel.: 01482-223344
Fax: 01482-593718.

Directions by Road:

M62 to Hull, then A63 into city. Pass cinema & ten pin bowling on right, and take next exit, signposted local traffic, infirmary. At roundabout, turn left into Hessle Road, and then right into Boulevard. Ground is on left, off Airlie Street. Street parking off the Boulevard.

Local Map:

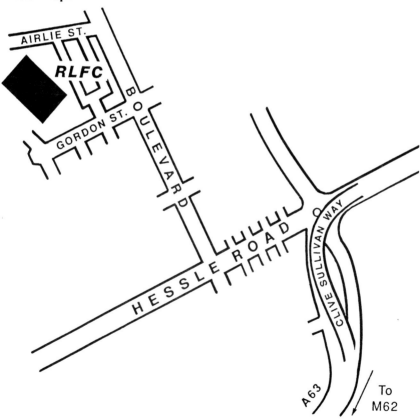

Keighley Cougars

Description of stadium: Scenic setting, next to cricket club and sports centre. Small main stand, and terracing, some covered.

Ground address: Cougar Park, Royd Ings Avenue, Keighley, W.Yorks BD21 3NB
Ground telephone No.: 01535-213111
Club Call: 0891-567575
Match day information: As above
Office address: As above
Office telephone No.: As above. **Fax:** 01535-213100
Ticket information phone no.: As above
Capacity: 5,500
Number of seats: 1,200
Advance ticket availability: Limited due to season ticket holders, but seats can be reserved by telephoning ground before match day.

Price reductions for:
Children: Yes
Age: Under 5s free
Pensioners: Yes
Unemployed: Yes with Passport to Leisure
Students: No
(Reduced prices for local "Passport to Leisure" holders)
Disabled: Yes

Disabled supporters:
Facilities: Ring above for details
Wheelchair access: Yes
Disabled toilets: Ring above for details
The Blind: Ring above for details

Club Shop:
Address: Cougar Shop, Cavendish Court, Keighley.
Telephone: 01535-210029
Match days: Small shop in ground open from 1.30 pm on match days

Supporters Club:
Address: Mr W. Dunford, 299, Valley Rd, Shipley BD18 2OO
Telephone : 01274-404584

Food and drink:
In the ground: Snack bars
Bars: In main stand

Transport:
Car parking: On nearby industrial estate

Public transport:
Nearest BR station: Keighley
Buses: Keighley Bus Station on
Lawkholme Lane. Bus: 78. Keighley
& District Travel: 01535-603284

Tourist Information:
Haworth Tourist Information
Centre, 2-4 West Lane, Haworth, Nr
Keighley, W.Yorkshire, BD22 8EF.
Tel.: 01535-642329.
Fax: 01535-647721.

Directions by Road:

From west: M62 take junction 24, A629 signposted Halifax. Stay on A629 to Keighley. Turn right at roundabout, and straight over second roundabout, to join A650 in Keighley. Ground is on A650 on the left. Main entrance on Royd Ings Avenue, on right off A650.

From east: M62 take junction 26, M606 to Bradford. Take A6177 (fifth exit), and turn left onto A650. Stay on A650, then as above.

Local Map:

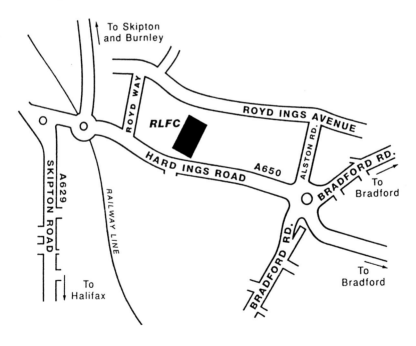

Rochdale Hornets

Description of ground: Shared with Rochdale FC. Modern main stand, cover behind one goal and on side.

Ground address: Spotland Stadium, Sandy Lane, Rochdale, Lancashire.
Ground telephone No.: 01706-48004
Club Call: None
Match day information: As above
Office address: P.O. Box 48, Rochdale OL16 1PE
Office telephone No.: As above
Ticket information phone no.: As above
Capacity: 7,500
Number of seats: 1,850
Advance ticket availability: Yes

Price reductions for:
Children: Yes
Age: Under 12
Pensioners: Yes
Unemployed: No
Students: No
Disabled: Yes

Disabled supporters:
Facilities: Bars accessible
Wheelchair access: Viewing area for 18 wheelchairs
Disabled toilets: Yes
The blind: No special facilities

Club Shop: Commercial Office
Address: As above
Telephone: As above
Opening hours: 9.30am - 5.00pm
Match days: 12.00 noon - 3.00pm and 4.30-5.00pm

Supporters Club:
Address: Mr G.Bargh 44, Ellis Fold, Norden Rochdale OL12 7RR
Telephone Number: 01706-44047

Food and drink:
In the ground: Kiosks
Bars: Spotland suite open to visitors. Snacks & meals from 1.00 pm.

Transport:
Car parking: Car park in stadium (£1). Also side street parking.
Public transport:
Nearest BR station: Rochdale station (1.5 miles)
Buses: R1, R2, R3 or 459.

General Facilities:
Suite can be hired for private parties.

Tourist Information:
Rochdale Tourist Information Centre, The Clock Tower, Town Hall, Rochdale, Lancashire, OL16 1AB.
Tel.: 01706-356592

Directions by Road:
From east or west: Take M62 to junction 20, A627(M) to Rochdale. Turn left at roundabout onto A664, and at next roundabout take second turnoff, B6452, Roch Valley Way. Stay on B6452, cross B6222 (Bury Road), B6452 now becomes Sandy Lane. Ground is on right-hand side. Street parking before reaching ground.

Local Map:

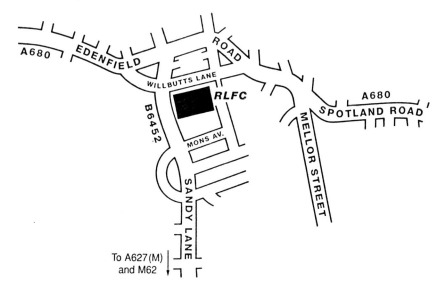

43

Salford Reds

Description of ground: Main stand on one side, covered terracing on other. Large stand behind one goal. Further ground development planned.

Ground address: The Pavilion, Willows Road, Salford, Lancs M5 2FQ
Ground telephone No.: 0161-737-6363
Club Call: 0891-121644
Match day information: 0891-121644
Office address: As above
Office telephone No.: 0161-736-6564 (3 lines)   **Fax:** 0161-745-8072
Ticket information phone no.: 0161-736-6564
Capacity: 11,500
Number of seats: 2,500
Advance ticket availability: Yes

Price reductions for:
Children: Yes
Age: Up to 16
Pensioners: Yes
Unemployed: No
Students: Yes
(advance sales only)
Disabled: No

Disabled supporters:
Facilities: Viewing area. Free admission to wheelchair users on reporting to Secretary's office.
Wheelchair access: Yes
Disabled toilets: Yes
The blind: Yes (no audio facilities)

Club Shop: Red Devils "Tackle" Shop in Salford City shopping complex. Also shop at ground.
Address: As for club

Telephone: 0161-745-7898
Opening hours: 10.00am - 4.00pm
Monday to Saturday
Match days: 1.30pm to 6.30pm
(Shop at ground only)

Supporters Club:
Address: Mr S.White, c/o Club

Food and drink:
In the ground: Various catering kiosks.
Bars: Willows open to visitors on match days. No admission charge
Restaurant: Three course meals available. Check before game on office phone number.

Transport:
Car parking: In school at top of road (£1).

Public transport: Information: 0161-228-7811

Nearest BR station: Eccles or Pendleton. Metro link being constructed.

Buses: 70, 71, 73, 74.

General Facilities:

The Willows Cabaret Venue.

Details: 0161-736-8541

Tourist Information:

Manchester Visitor Centre, Town Hall Extension, Lloyd Street, Manchester M60 2lA.

Tel.: 0161-234-3157/8.

Fax: 0161-236-9900.

Directions by road:

From east or west: Take M62 to junction 12, then M602. At first junction, take first exit, A576, and bear left. Follow road round, past fourth set of traffic lights, to top of hill. Turn right into Weaste Lane, B5228, and ground is on right.

From Manchester: Take A6 from city centre, turn left onto A576, then left into Weaste Lane, B5228, and ground is on right.

Local Map:

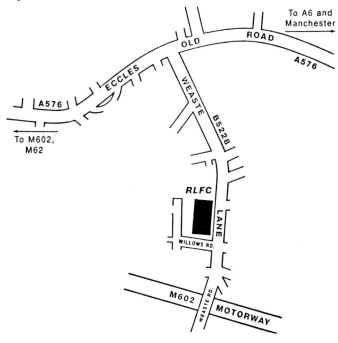

Wakefield Trinity

Description of ground: Main stand on one side., opne terracing behind one goal, social club behind other one. Limited capacity adequate for first division, but club have plans to find new stadium.

Ground address: Belle Vue, Doncaster Rd, Wakefield, WF1 5HT
Ground telephone No.: 01924-290243
Club Call: 0898-888659
Match day information: 01924-372445 (from 1.30pm)
Office address: George Street, Wakefield W. Yorks WF1 1NE
Office telephone No.: 01924-372445
Ticket information phone no.: 01924-372445
Capacity: 8,000
Number of seats: 1,600
Advance ticket availability: Yes for seats

Price reductions for:
Children: Yes
Pensioners: Yes
Unemployed: No
Students: No
Disabled: Yes

Disabled supporters:
Facilities: Viewing area and parking on request
Wheelchair access: Yes
Disabled toilets: Yes
The blind: No special facilities

Club Shop:
Address: George Street, Wakefield WF1 1NE
Telephone: 01924-372445
Opening hours: 9.00 am - 5.30pm
Match days: 1.30pm - 3.30pm at rear of stand, also programme hut.

Supporters Club: Open 1.30 pm to 5.00 pm match days
Address: Mr N.Vause, 124, Doles Crescent, Royston S71 4LB
Telephone number: 01226-723845

Food and drink:
In the ground: Yes - kiosks
Bars: Yes

Transport:
Car parking: No
Public transport: Information: 0113-245-7676.
Nearest BR station: Agbrigg
Buses: Mini Bus: 100, 104.
Others: 122, 123, 145, 148, 149, 150, 485 & 498

General Facilities:
Coach house bar and carvery meals. Supporters Club snack bar. Super Bowl next door to ground.

Tourist Information:

Wakefield Tourist Information Centre, Town Hall, Wood Street, Wakefield, W.Yorks WF1 2HQ. Tel: 01924-295000/1. Fax: 01924-295283.

Directions by Road:
From west: M62 to junction 29, then M1 south to junction 41. Take A650, then A61 to town centre. After town centre, fork left onto A638, and ground is on right. To avoid M62/M1 junction, leave M62 at junction 28, take A653, then A650 to Wakefield.
From east: M62 take junction 30, A642 to town centre. Turn left at roundabout onto A61, then as for west above.
From north: M1 to junction 41, then as for west above.
From south: M1 to junction 39, take A636 signposted Wakefield. Turn right onto A638, then right onto A61, then as for west above.

Local Map:

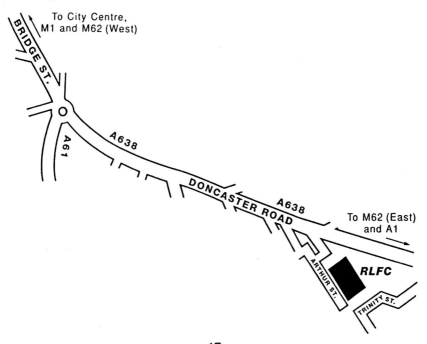

47

Whitehaven Warriors

Description of ground: Stand on one side, covered terracing behind one goal. Open terracing otherwise.

Ground address: Recreation Ground, Coach Road, Whitehaven
Ground telephone No.: 01946-692915
Club Call: None
Match day information: As above
Office address: 5, Roper Street Whitehaven, CA28 7AU
Office telephone No.: 01946-622915
Ticket information phone no.: As above
Capacity: 6,000
Number of seats: 500
Advance ticket availability: None

Price reductions for:
Children: Yes
Age: Free to under 16s
Pensioners: Yes
Unemployed: No
Students: Yes
Disabled: Yes

Disabled supporters:
Facilities: Viewing area by arrangement. Bars accessible
Wheelchair access: Yes
Disabled toilets: Yes
The blind: No special facilities

Club Shop:
Address: 5, Roper Street, Whitehaven
Telephone: 01946-692915 (Tanya Clark)
Opening hours: 9.00am -5.00pm

(Closed 1.00 pm to 2.00 pm)
Match days: Yes

Supporters Club:
Address: Avon Bar, Recreation Ground, Whitehaven
Telephone number: 01946-691113

Food and drink:
In the ground: Yes
Bars: Avon Bar. Membership Card admits free entrance.

Transport:
Car parking: At ground
Public transport:
Nearest BR station: Information: 01228-44711 or 01229-820805. Corkickle Station (Closed Sundays & evenings. Infrequent service). Whitehaven station (limited Sunday

service from Carlisle only).
Buses: 01,02, 7/9, 9/7, 09, 12, 17 all stop near ground.
Information: 01946-63222.

Tourist Information:
Whitehaven Tourist Information Centre, Market Hall, Market Place, Whitehaven, Cumbria CA28 7JG. Tel: 01946-695678.

General Facilities:
Free creche facilities on matchdays.
Free after match entertainment

Directions by Road:
M6 take junction 40, A66 signposted Keswick. After passing Keswick and Cockermouth, turn left onto A595. Stay on A595, pass first junction with A5094. Turn right at traffic lights into A5094 (Inkerman Terrace), left into Coach Road, and ground is on left.
N.B. The A66 may be very busy during the summer.

Local Map:

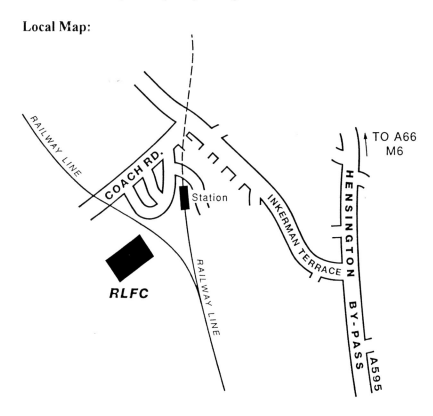

Widnes

Description of ground: Small main stand, covered terracing behind one goal and other side. Ground of disparate parts, reflecting piecemeal development, and not reflecting the club's achievements on the pitch over the years.

Ground address: Naughton Park, Lowerhouse Lane, Widnes,WA8 7DZ
Ground telephone No.: 0151-495-2250
Club Call: 0891-888-633
Match day information: 0151-495-2250
Office address: As above
Office telephone No.: 0151-495-2250. Fax: 0151-423-2720
Ticket information phone no.: 0151-495-2250
Capacity: 14,500
Number of seats: 1,300
Advance ticket availability: Yes

Price reductions for:
Children: Yes
Age: School age
Pensioners: Yes
Unemployed: No
Students: No
Disabled: No

Disabled supporters:
Facilities: Viewing area
Wheelchair access: Yes
Disabled toilets: Yes
The blind: No special facilities

Club Shop:
Address: As above
Telephone: As above
Opening hours: Monday to Friday 9.00 am to 5.00 pm
Match days: 2 hours before match and 1 hour afterwards

Supporters Club:
*Address:*Ms H.Richards, "Oakwood", Cronton Rd, Tarback, Prescot L35 1QU
Tel: 0151-423-5882

Food and drink:
In the ground: Kiosks
Bars: Social Club £1 admission

Transport:
Car parking: Some at ground
Public transport: Information: 0151-236-7676
Nearest BR station: Widnes
Buses:
Information: 0151-423-3333.
2 (not Sunday), 5 (Sunday only),

12 (not Sunday) , 14.
North Western buses:
01928-572221.
H26, H30, T4, T10 to Town Centre.
None on Sundays.

Tourist Information:
Liverpool Tourist Information, Merseyide Welcome Centre, Clayton Square, Shopping Centre, Liverpool, Merseyside, L1 1QR.
Tel: 0151-709-3631.

Directions by Road:
From north, east or west: M62 take junction 7, then A568. Stay on A568 bypassing town centre, and come off onto A562 (Ashley Way). Go straight across two roundabouts into Lowerhouse Lane, and ground is on right.
From south: M6 junction 20, M56 west. M56 junction 12 take A557 signposted Runcorn and Widnes. Join A533 signposted Widnes, cross Runcorn Bridge, then turn off onto A562. Then as above.
N.B. If the M62 is busy, using the M56 as above may be quicker.

Local Map:

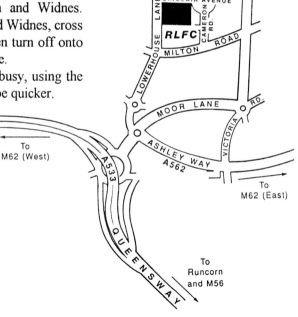

York

Description of ground: Athletics stadium, with main stand on one side, and covered terracing on other. York's home since 1989, when their previous ground was sold.

Ground address: Jockey Lane, Huntington, York YO3 9XX
Ground telephone No.: 01904-634636
Club Call: None
Match day information: As above after 1.30pm
Office address: As above
Office telephone No.: As above. **Fax:** 01904-629049
Ticket information phone no.: As above
Capacity: 5,000
Number of seats: 800
Advance ticket availability: Yes

Price reductions for:
Children: Yes
Age: Under 16
Pensioners: Yes
Unemployed: No
Students: No
Disabled: Yes

Disabled supporters:
Facilities: Disabled viewing area
Wheelchair access: Yes
Disabled toilets: Yes
The blind: No special facilities

Club Shop:
Address: As above
Telephone: As above
Opening hours: 9.30 am to 4.30 pm
Match days: 1 hour before kick off and 15 minutes after

Supporters Club:
Address: Mr P.Grainger, 26, Howe Hill, Close, York YO2 4SN

Food and drink:
In the ground: 2 kiosks
Bars: Not open to visiting supporters

Transport:
Car parking: 100 cars
Public transport: Service bus from York railway station. Leaves at 2.30 pm arrives at Stadium 2.55 pm. Departs from stadium at 4.55 pm and 5.55 pm.
Nearest BR station: York. 3 miles away
Buses: See above

General Facilities: Sports centre at stadium. Swimming pool being built.

Tourist Information:

York Tourist Information Centre, 6, Rougier Street, York, N.Yorks, YO2 1JA.
Tel.: 01904-620557.
Fax: 01904-620756.

Directions by Road:

From south and west: A1 then A64 towards York. Stay on the A64, and at roundabout with A1237, take A1237. Immediately at roundabout, turn onto A1036 towards York. At roundabout turn right into Jockey Lane, left at next roundabout, and left into Kathryn Avenue for stadium. It is well signposted from A1036.

From north: A1, turn onto A1237, then as above. N.B. A1237 is not dual carriageway, and may be busy during the summer.

From east: A64, then as for south and west

Local Map:

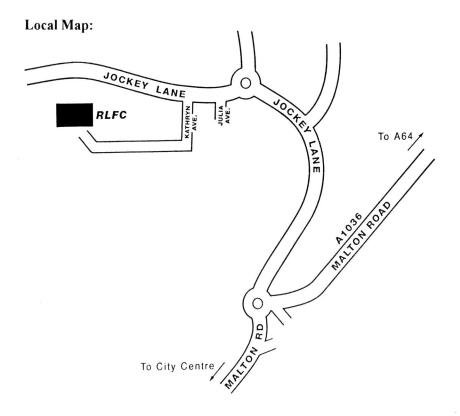

New stand at Batley

Dewsbury's Crown Flatt stadium

One of the game's traditional homes - Featherstone Rovers

Huddersfield's "Big Mac" - Australia v New Zealand World Cup semi-final

Hull's famous Threepenny stand

Keighley's message to the world: "Get Cougarised"

56

The Willows, Weaste, home of Salford Reds

A scenic view - Whitehaven

Widnes - a club with a great history

The main stand at York's Ryedale Stadium

The Second Division

Barrow Braves
Bramley
Carlisle Raiders
Chorley Chieftans
Doncaster Dragons
Highfield
Hull Kingston Rovers
Hunslet Hawks
Leigh Centurions
Swinton

The main stand at Barrow

Barrow Braves

Description of the ground: Main stand on one side, covered terracing on other side and behind both goals. In close proximity of the shipyard that is the mainstay of the town's economy. Very near town centre.

Ground address: Craven Park, Duke Street, Barrow in Furness LA14 5UW
Ground telephone No.: 01229-830470
Club Call: None
Match day information: 1229-820273(Office) or 830470(Ground)
Office address: 78, Scott Street Barrow in Furness, LA14 1QE
Office telephone No.: 01229-820273
Ticket information phone no.: 01229-824454
Capacity: 7,000
Number of seats: 1,000
Advance ticket availability: Not usually

Price reductions for:
Children: Yes
Age: Up to 14
Pensioners: Yes
Unemployed: Yes
Students: No
Disabled: No

Disabled supporters:
Facilities: None
Wheelchair access: No
Disabled toilets: No
The Blind: No special facilities

Club Shop:
Address: Rugby Shop, 78, Scott Street, Barrow in Furness, LA14 1QE
Also: Shop inside ground open on match days (Not currently open)

Telephone:
Rugby Shop: 01229-824454
Opening hours: 9-5 Monday to Wednesday, 9-3 Thursday, 9-4 Friday, 9.30 - 12 midday Saturday

Food and drink:
In the ground: Snack bars
Bars: Fatty's - Hindpool Road

Travel:
Car parking: None at ground. Street parking available
Public transport:
Nearest BR station: Barrow (Abbey Road). (NB Very limited Sunday services)
Buses: Most stop at the Town Hall, a few minutes walk from the ground, including 1, 1A, 2, 3, 3A, 4, 4A, 5,

7, 9, 10, 11, 12, 503, 509, 518, 530, 531, 535, 730, 735, X35.

Tourist Information:

Forum 28, Duke Street, Barrow in

Furness, Cumbria LA14 1HU
Tel.: 01229-870156
Fax: 01229-432289

Directions by road:

From M6: Take junction 36, and follow A590, following signs for Barrow. Road runs direct to Barrow. Pass ASDA supermarket. Turn left into Duke Street, and ground is on right, opposite further education college.

N.B. Although most of this road is dual carriageway, it can be very busy in the summer. Allow at least one and a half hours from the M6. Grange over Sands is a nice place to stop for a meal on the way, about 2 miles off the A590.

Local Map:

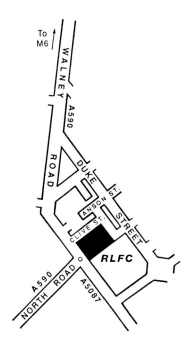

Bramley

Description of ground: Leeds RUFC ground. Main stand on one side, small stand on other. Grass bank behind one goal, club house behind other. At time of writing, no sign for Bramley RLFC at ground.

Ground address: Leeds RUFC, Clarence Field, Commercial Road, Leeds LS5
Ground telephone No.: 0113-275-5029
Club Call: None
Match day information: 0113-275-5029
Office address: As above
Office telephone No.: As above
Ticket Information Phone No.: As above
Capacity: 4,000
Number of seats: 1,000
Advance ticket availability: No

Price reductions for:
Children: Yes
Age: Under 13
Pensioners: Yes
Unemployed: Yes: No:
Students: Yes: No:
Disabled: Yes:

Disabled supporters:
Facilities: None
Wheelchair access: Yes
Disabled toilets: No
The Blind: No special facilities

Club Shop:
Address: As above, c/o Supporters Club
Telephone: None
Opening hours: Match days only

Supporters Club: Steve Hunter
Address: c/o Club
Telephone Number: As above

Food and drink:
In the ground: In club house
Bars: In club house

Transport:
Car parking: Free. In ground and side streets.
Public transport:
Information: 0113-245-7676
Nearest BR station: Headingley
Buses: 41 from Eastgate, to junction Commercial Road with Bridge Road.
Also 73 and 91 go by ground.

Directions by road:

From west: Take M62 junction 27, M621 towards Leeds. Turn left at junction 2 onto A643. Turn right at roundabout towards A58(M), immediately turn left onto A65 (Kirkstall Road), signposted Ilkley. Stay on A65, which becomes Commercial Road. At traffic lights, turn left into Bridge Road, and ground is on left. Sign for Leeds RUFC, there is no sign for Bramley RLFC.

From east or south: Take M62 junction 29, then M1 north to junction 47, then M621 to junction 2, then as above.

N.B. For people familiar with travelling to Headingley, drive down Kirstall Lane away from Otley Road. Pass Headingley on the left, and cross the A65 into Bridge Road. Ground is on left.

N.B. At the time of writing, Bramley were still playing at Clarence Field, and we believe will be for the 1996 season. However, there are building plans for this ground, so check with the club, the press or the Rugby League.

Local map:

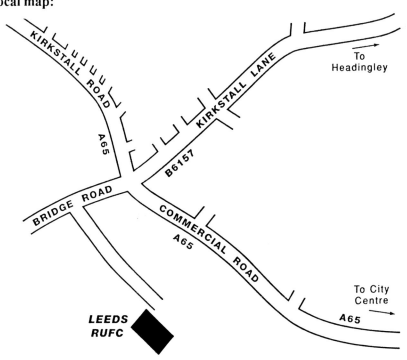

63

Carlisle Raiders

Description of ground: Stand on one side, covered terracing on the other. New stand behind one goal. Club have made considerable improvements since moving to the ground.

Ground address: Gillford Park, Petteril Bank Road, Carlisle, CA1 3AF
Ground telephone No.:01228-401212
Club Call: None
Match day information: 01228-401212
Office address: As above
Office telephone No.:01228-401212
Ticket information phone no.:01228-401212
Capacity: 4,000
Number of seats: 750
Advance ticket availability: Yes

Price reductions for:
Children: Yes - Half price
Age: Under 16
Pensioners: Yes -Half price
Unemployed: Yes - Half price
Students: Yes - Half price
*Disabled:*No

Disabled supporters:
Facilities: Yes
Wheelchair access: Yes
(ramp to stand)
Disabled toilets: Yes
The blind: Yes

Club Shop:
Address: As above (at ground)
Telephone: As above
Opening hours: On match days

Food and drink:
*In the ground:*Various pies, crisps, chocloate etc
Bars: Two

Transport:
Car parking: At ground and street parking
Public transport:
Nearest BR station: Carlisle Citadel station (1.5 miles from ground)
Buses: 62 (Very limited Sunday service). Information: 01946-63222.

General Facilities:
Function room available

Tourist Information:
Carlisle Visitor Centre,
Old Town Hall, Green Market,
Cumbria CA3 8JH
Tel: 01228-512444,
Fax: 01228-511758

Directions by Road:
Take M6 junction 42, then A6 towards Carlisle. Turn left into Petteril Bank Road, and ground is on right, at bottom of road, signposted Gillford Park..
From town centre: Take A6, then turn right into Petteril Bank Road, and ground is on right, at bottom of road, signposted Gillford Park.

Local Map:

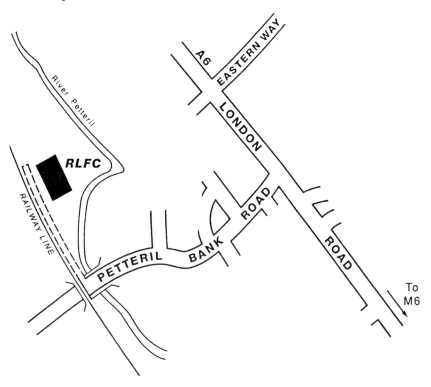

Chorley Chieftans

Description of ground: Chorley Football Club's Ground. Main stand on one side, cover behind both goals. Social Club at entrance to ground. Near town centre. Not to be confused with Leyland Motors football ground in Duke Street, where the club used to play.

Ground address: Victory Park, Duke Street, Chorley PR7 3DU
Ground telephone No.: 01257-232116
Club Call: None
Match day information: 01257-232116 or 01257-263406
Office address: Victory Park, Duke Street, Chorley, Lancs PR7 3DU
Office telephone No.: As above
Ticket information phone no.: 01257-232116
Capacity: 9,900
Number of seats: 700
Advance ticket availability: Not usually

Price reductions for:
Children: Yes
Pensioners: Yes
Unemployed: No
Students: No
Disabled: Yes

Disabled supporters:
Facilities: None
Wheelchair access: No
Disabled toilets: No
The Blind: No special facilities

Club Shop:
Address: As above
Opening hours: Match days

Supporters Club:
Address: c/o Chorley RLFC.

Food and drink:
In the Ground: Snack bars
Bars: Social Club in the ground open before and after matches, also midweek evenings.

Transport:
Car parking: Limited at ground. Street parking available.
Public transport:
Nearest BR station: Chorley (1/4 mile from ground)
Buses: Stop 15 minutes walk from ground on Bolton Road. Run from Wigan, Bolton and Chorley Circular service.

General Facilities:
Social Club by entrance. Hot and cold food and bar.

Tourist Information:

Bolton Tourist Information Centre, Town Hall, Victory Square, Bolton, Lancs, BL1 1RU.
Tel.: 01204-364333.
Fax: 01204-398101.

Directions by Road:
From east: M62 take junction 14 - M61 north. Junction 6 take A6 to Chorley. Turn left into Pilling Lane, and right into Ashby Street.
From west and south: M6 take junction 27, A5029 towards Wigan. At junction with A49, go straight across onto B5239. Turn left onto A5106, and left onto A6. Then as above.
From north: M6 junction 30 take M61 south. Junction 8 take A6 south, after roundabout turn right into Pilling Lane, than as above.

Local Map:

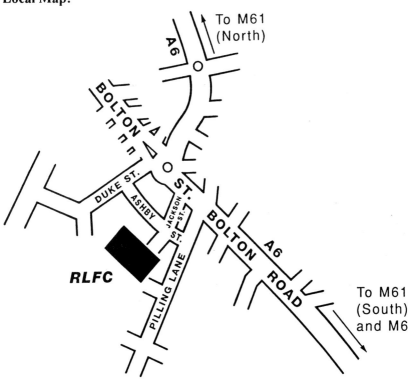

Doncaster Dragons

Ground address: Regal Meadow Court Stadium, Station Road, Stainforth, Doncaster DN7 5HS
Ground telephone No.: 01302-350400
Club Call: None
Match day information: As above
Office address: As above
Office telephone No.: As above
Ticket information phone no.: As above
Capacity: 3,000 plus overspill area
Number of seats: None
Advance ticket availability: No

Price reductions for:
Children: Yes
Age: Under 14
Pensioners: Yes
Unemployed: No
Students: No
Disabled: No

Disabled supporters:
Facilities:
Wheelchair access: Yes
Disabled toilets: Yes
The Blind: Yes

Club Shop:
Address: As above
Telephone: As above
Opening hours: 10 am to 4 pm
Match Days: 10 am to after match

Supporters Club:
Address: Mrs K. Wilson, 15, Marsh Rd, Bentley, Doncaster
Telephone: 01302-788400

Food and drink:
In the ground: Cafe and restaurant
Bars: 4

Transport:
Car parking: 450 places
Public transport: Information: 01302-344949 or 01709-515151
Nearest BR station: Hatfield & Stainforth
Buses: 250 (Sunday only from Moorends), 182 (not Sunday), 183. From Southern Bus Station, College Road, Doncaster

General facilities:
Regular greyhound racing. Executive suites for hire.

Tourist Information:
Doncaster Tourist Information
Centre, Central Library, Waterdale,
Doncaster, S.Yorks DN1 3JE.
Tel.: 01302-734309.
Fax: 01302-735385

Directions by road:

From north, west or east: M62 take junction 35 M18 south. Junction 6 take A614 south, turn right at junction with M180 onto A18. Take A18 to Hatfield, tun right into Station Road. Stay on Station Road and ground is on left hand side after the railway bridge on the outskirts of Stainforth. (This is more direct than taking the A1 or A19 from the west, which would involve going through Doncaster). There is a sign for the stadium on Station Road.

From south: A1(M) junction 35 take M18 to junction 5. Then take M180 to junction 1. Come off onto A18. Turn right onto A18, then as above.

Local map:

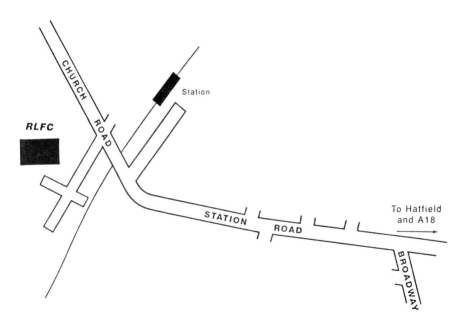

Highfield

Description of ground: Main stand on one side, open terracing otherwise. Stand currently not in use.

Ground address: Highfield RLFC, Prescot FC, Eaton Street, Prescot, Merseyside L34
Ground telephone No.: 0151-430-0507 Fax: 0151-5225-6546
Club Call: None
Match day information: 0151-430-0507
Office address: Eaton Street, Prescot, Merseyside L34
Office telephone No.: 0151-430-0507, Fax: 0151-525-6546
Secretary: 0151-523-4233
Ticket information phone no.: Contact club
Capacity: 2,300
Number of seats: 800
Advance ticket availability: If necessary

Price reductions for:
Children: Yes
Pensioners: Yes
Unemployed: Being considered
Students: No
Disabled: No

Disabled supporters:
Facilities: Separate gate
Wheelchair access: Yes
Disabled toilets: No
The blind: No special facilities

Club Shop:
Address: Awaiting premises

Supporters Club:
Address: None

Food and drink:
In the ground: Yes
Bars: Club house under stand

Transport:
Car parking: Free in surrounding streets. Municipal car parks 5 minutes walk from ground. Coaches - park at Prescot Centre.
Public transport: Information: Mersey Travel 0151-236-7676
Nearest BR station: Prescot
Buses: On main bus route from Warrington, St. Helens & Liverpool.
Buses: 7, 10, 10A, 10X, 14A, 34, 48, 50, 61, 89, 90, 90A, 106, 110, 161, 189, 195, 248, 289, 510.
(Many do not run on Sundays)

Tourist Information:
Liverpool Tourist Information, Merseyide Welcome Centre, Clayton Square, Shopping Centre, Liverpool, Merseyside, L1 1QR. Tel: 0151-709-3631.

Directions by Road:
From south, east or west: Take M62 to junction 6, then M57 to junction 2. At roundabout take A57 (Liverpool Road), and turn left into Hope Street. Ground is at end of street.
From north: Take M6 junction 24, A58 St Helens. Stay on A58 until junction with A57. At roundabout, turn left, and then right into High Street (still A57). Hope Street is on right.

Local Map:

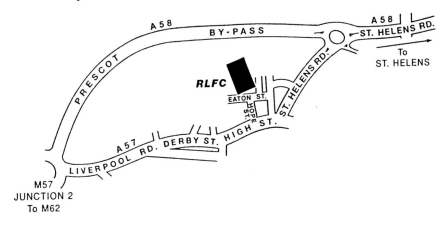

Hull Kingston Rovers

Description of ground: Modern stand on one side, large covered terrace on other. Terrace behind one goal. Stadium includes Speedway and Greyhound tracks. Reputedly very cold when wind blows in from river.

Ground address: Craven Park, Preston Rd, Hull, HU9 5HE
Ground telephone No.: 01482-374648
Club Call: None
Match day information: 01482-374648
Office address: Craven Park, Preston Road, Hull HU9 5HE
Office telephone No.: 01482-374648 Fax: 01482-791586
Ticket information phone no.: 01482-374648
Capacity: 9,500
Number of seats: 2,000
Advance ticket availability: 14 days in advance

Price reductions for:
Children: Yes
Age: Under 16. Under 5 - free
Pensioners: Yes
Unemployed: No
Students: Yes
(Advance tickets on production of students union card)
Disabled: Yes

Disabled supporters:
Facilities: Lift to restaurant and bar
Wheelchair access: Yes
Disabled toilets: Yes
The blind: No special facilities

Club Shop:
Address: As above.
Telephone: 01482-702726
Opening hours: 9.00am to

4.00 pm on weekdays
Match days: 2 hours before kick off

Supporters Club:
Address: Mr K.Longley 18, Bakewell Close, Greatfield Estate, Hull HU9 5LH
Telephone Number: 01482-374174

Food and drink:
In the ground: 3 refreshment bars
Bars: 2 bars

Transport:
Car parking: 900 places at ground
Public transport:
Nearest BR station: Hull Paragon
Buses: City Transport, EYMS from City. Buses: 24, 41, 43, 43B, 82.

General Facilities:

Match day meals in restaurant (pre booked)

Speedway racing at stadium every Wednesday (April to Oct) 7.30 pm

Greyhound racing Thursday and Saturday 7.30 pm

Private hire of facilities for parties, meetings and conferences available.

Tourist information:

City Information Service, Central Library, Albion Street, Hull, Humberside, HU1 3TF.

Tel.: 01482-223344

Fax: 01482-593718.

Directions by Road:

M62, then A63 into city. Stay on A63, and at roundabout turn right into Hedon Road, signposted Docks A63 (A1033). Turn left into Marfleet Avenue, and fork left into Marfleet Lane. Turn right into Preston Road, and ground is on right behind supermarket.

Local Map:

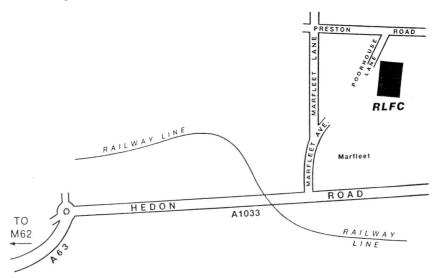

Hunslet Hawks

Description of stadium: Modern stand seating 2,471 people. No other development at present. Athletics stadium. Has facilitated the club's long awaited return to South Leeds, a few hundred yards from its original Parkside home.

Ground address: South Leeds Stadium, Middleton Grove, off Dewsbury Road, Leeds LS11 5DJ
Ground telephone No.: 0113-271-1675.
Club Call: 0891-440060
Match day information: As above
Office address: As above
Office telephone No.: 0113-271-1675. Fax: 0113-270-1198
Ticket information phone no.: As above
Capacity: 2,471
Number of seats: 2,471
Advance ticket availability: Yes

Price reductions for:
Children: Yes
Age: Under 16
Pensioners: Yes
Unemployed: No
Students: No
Disabled: Yes

Disabled supporters:
Facilities: Yes
Wheelchair access: Yes
Disabled toilets: Yes
The blind: No special facilities

Club Shop:
Address: As above
Telephone: As above
Opening hours: Weekdays 9.30 am to 5.00 pm
Match days: Before and after matches

Supporters Club:
Address: Peter Whitley 48, Southleigh Rd, Leeds LS11 5SG
Telephone: 0113-270-4505

Food and drink:
In the ground: Snack bars
Bars: 2 - 1 for members, 1 open to the public.

Transport:
Car parking: Free at stadium
Public transport: Information: 0113-245-7676

Nearest BR station: Leeds
Buses: 2, 3, 24, 25
(From Corn Exchange)

General Facilities:
Leisure centre and banqueting suite
at stadium

Tourist Information:
The Regional Travel Centre, The
Arcade, City Station, Leeds,
W.Yorkshire, LS1 1PL.
Tel.: 0113-247-8301/2.
Fax: 0113-247-8306

Directions by Road:
From south, east and west: M1 take
junction 45, turn left onto Tunstall
Road. Turn left onto Dewsbury
Road, and left into Middleton
Grove. Ground is on left hand side
past industrial estates.
From city centre: Take A653
signposted Dewsbury, then as
above.

Local Map:

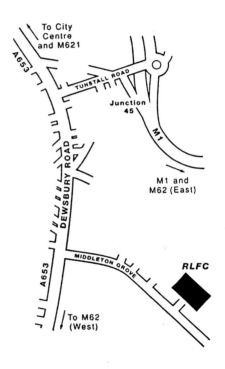

Leigh Centurions

Description of ground: Small main stand, covered terrace and stand on other side. Now surrounded by supermarkets, and next to the Leigh East ARLFC ground.

Ground address: Hilton Park, Kirkhall Lane, Leigh, Lancs WN7 1RN
Ground telephone No.: 01942-743743
Club Call: 0891-122712
Match day information: As above
Office address: As above
Office telephone No.: As above. **Fax:** 01942-261843
Ticket information phone no.: As above
Capacity: 9,240
Number of seats: 1,425
Advance ticket availability: Stand tickets only

Price reductions for:
Children: Yes
Age: Under 16
Pensioners: Yes
Unemployed: No
Students: No
Disabled: Yes. Wheelchair Users free

Disabled supporters:
Facilities: Designated area. Bar accessible.
Wheelchair access: At players entrance
Disabled toilets: One special. Other toilets accessible
The blind: No

Club Shop:
Address: As above.
*Telephone:*01942-743743
Opening hours: 8.30 am to 5.00 pm Monday to Friday
Match days: From 1.00 pm to 3.00 pm, and for short time after game

Supporters Club:
Address: Mr D.Disley, 104, Windermere Rd, Leigh, WN7 1UZ
Telephone number: None

Food and drink:
In the ground: Snack bars
Bars: Bars open to visitors. Supporters club membership card accepted as free admission to bars.

Transport:
Car parking: Small area at ground. Street parking.
Public transport:
Information: 0161-228-7811
Nearest BR station: Atherton
Buses: Along Leigh Road: 35, 516, 582, 583, 594, 595, 652, 658, 670, 685, 697

Tourist Information:
Wigan Tourist Information Office, Trencherfield Mill, Wallgate, Lancashire, WN3 4EL.
Tel: 01942-825677.
Fax: 01942-828540.

Directions by Road:
From east: M62, junction 14, take A580 (East Lancashire Road), turn right onto A579. Follow A579, passing junctions with A572 and A578. Ground is visible on right, turn right into Kirkhall Lane. Ground is behind superstore. Turn right down side of superstore, or into Glebe Street.
From north or west: M6, junction 23, take A580 east towards Manchester. Turn left into A572, then left into A579, then as above.

Local Map:

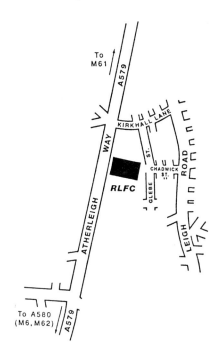

Swinton

Description of ground: Bury FC ground. Mainly seated stadium, having had considerable modernisation programme over last couple of years.

Ground address: Gigg Lane, Bury, Lancashire BL9 9HR
Ground telephone No.: 0161-761-2328
Club Call: 0891-888-660
Match day information: As above
Office address: As above
Office telephone No.: As above
Ticket information phone no.: 0161-794-6150
Capacity: 12,500
Number of seats: 10,000
Advance ticket availability: No

Price reductions for:
Children: Yes
Age: Free up to 12 years
Pensioners: Yes
Unemployed: No
Students: No
Disabled: Yes
Free admission for wheelchair users

Disabled supporters:
Facilities: Designated area.
Wheelchair access: Yes
Disabled toilets: Yes
The blind: No special facilities

Club Shop:
Address: 112 Station Road, Swinton M27 6BT
Telephone: 0161-794-6150
Opening hours: Monday to Friday.: 9.00 am to 5.00 pm

Saturday: 10.00 am to 12 noon
Match days: At gound 1.30 pm to 3.00 pm.

Supporters Club:
Address: c/o John Kidd
01706-212258

Food and drink:
In the ground: Snackbars both sides of ground.
Bars: Social club open before and after match 0161-764-6771

Transport:
Car parking: £1.00
Public transport: Information: 0161-228-7811
Nearest BR station: Town centre
Metrolink 1 mile from ground
Buses: From town centre, stop at

Gigg Lane. 90, 92, 93, 134, 135, 136, 137, 138, 139, 495, 520, 524, 743, 790. Disabled access buses: 975, 976, 978.

General Facilities: Social club at ground.

Tourist Information:
Bury Tourist Information Centre, The Met Arts Centre, Market Street, Lancashire, BL9 0BN.
Tel.: 0161-705-5111.
Fax.: 0161-705-5919.

Directions by Road:
From east or west: Take M62 to junction 17, then A56 (signposted Whitefield or Bury). Pass junction with A6053, and Gigg Lane is on right, opposite playing fields. Not well signposted.
From Bury Town Centre: Take A56, and Gigg Lane is on left.
(N.B. Ignore M66 which is signposted Bury from M62. Above route is more straightforward)

Local Map:

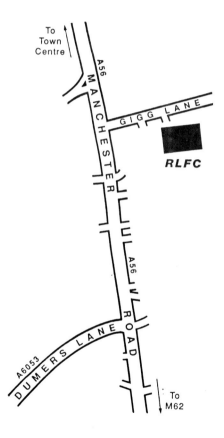

Carlisle's new stand

Rugby League and football together - Chorley's Victory Park

The Meadow Court Stadium - Doncaster Dragons' new home

Another new home - Hull Kingston Rover's Craven Park

Home at last - Hunslet back in south Leeds

Gigg Lane: another shared ground - Swinton and Bury FC

International Grounds

Elland Road, Leeds United FC
Gateshead International Stadium
Ninian Park, Cardiff City FC
Old Trafford, Manchester United FC
The Vetch Field, Swansea City FC
Wembley Stadium

Elland Road - a regular venue for international matches

Elland Road, Leeds United Football Club

Description of ground: Modern all seater stadium, including enormous new stand on one side.

Ground address: Elland Road, Leeds LS11 OES
Ground telephone No.: 0113-271 0637
Capacity: 39,896
Number of seats: as above

Disabled supporters:
Facilities: Yes
Wheelchair access: Room for 27 in North Stand and 6 in West Stand
Disabled toilets: In all areas
The Blind: 50 seats with commentary in South West stand

(short walk to ground)
Public transport: Information: 0113-245-7676
Nearest BR station: Leeds City (1.5 miles)
Buses: 93 and 96, plus special match day services.

Food and drink:
In the ground: Good choice of hot and cold snacks

Transport:
Car Parking: Low Fields Road

Tourist Information:
Regional Travel Centre, The Arcade, City Station, Leeds, W.Yorkshire, LS1 1PL.
Tel.: 0113-2478301/2.
Fax: 0113-2478036

Directions by road: *From west:* M62, take junction 27 - M621. Take junction 2, A643 and turn right. Stadium is on right, parking available on left hand side. *From south :* M1 to junction 47, take M621, junction 2 then as above. *From east:* M62 to junction 29, M1 north, then as from south.

Local map: See page 90

Gateshead International Stadium

Description of ground: All seater stadium with 3,300 covered seats in main stand. Home of the Gateshead Aacademy team. Disabled facilities will be expanded during 1996.

Ground address: International Stadium, Neilson Rd, Gateshead NE10 OEF
Ground telephone No.: 0191-478-1687
Capacity: 12,000
Number of seats: 12,000

Disabled supporters:
Facilities: Yes
Wheelchair access: Yes - at front of stand
Disabled toilets: Yes
The Blind: No special facilities

Food and drink: One bar. Hot and cold snacks available

Transport:
Car Parking: Yes, 3,500 places
Public Transport:
Information: 0191-232-5325.
Gateshead Stadium Metro station
Nearest BR station:

Newcastle Central
Buses: 93 or 94
No direct buses from Newcastle City centre. Use metro service.

General facilities: Athletics stadium with various sports facilities.

Tourist information:
Gateshead Tourist Information Centre, Metrocentre, Portcullis, 7,The Arcade, Tyne and Wear NE11 9YL
Tel: 0191-460-6345
Fax: 0191-460-4285

Directions by road:
From south: A1/A1(M) towards Newcastle. After Washington services, take A194(M). Turn left onto A184, towards centre of Gateshead. Turn right into Neilson Road, and stadium is on right.
From Carlisle: A69 towards Newcastle, then take A1 south, and turn onto A184. Stay on A184, and turn left into Neilson Road.

Local map: See page 91

Ninian Park, Cardiff City Football Club

Description of ground: Seating on two sides, and behind one goal. Standing behind other goal. On the edge of the city - limited pubs, places to eat and shops near the ground.

Ground address: Ninian Park, Sloper Road, Cardiff CF1 8SX
Ground telephone No.: 01222-398636
Capacity: 13,695
Number of seats: 11,370

Disabled supporters:
Facilities: Yes
Wheelchair access: Enclosure for 20 at pitch level
Disabled toilets: In main stand
The Blind: On request

athleitcs stadium
Public Transport: Information:
Nearest BR station: Ninian Park. Cardiff Central (one mile)
Bus: no.1 from main station. 12 & 13 to Sloper Road.

Food and drink:
In the ground: Snack bars

Transport:
Car parking: Large car park opposite Ninian Park, entrance by

Tourist Information:
Cardiff Tourist Information, Central Station, Penarth Road, Cardiff CF1 1QY
Tel: 01222-227281

Directions by road:

From M4: Take junction 33, A4232 towards city centre. Pass junction with A48, then left onto B4267, Leckwith Road. Athletics stadium is on right, with access to Ninian Park car parking. This route avoids the city centre.

Local Map: See page 91

Old Trafford, Manchester United FC

Description of ground: Modern all-seater stadium. Includes two "super-stores" and Manchester United museum.

Ground address: Sir Matt Busby Way, Old Trafford, Manchester M16 ORA
Ground telephone No.: 0161- 872-1661
Capacity: 55,000 (by end 1996)
Number of seats: as above

Disabled supporters:
Facilities: Yes
Wheelchair access: 37 places
Disabled toilets: Yes
The Blind: 20 seats in South East Quadrant with commentary

Food and drink:
Bars and snack bars

Transport:
Car Parking: Multi-storey car park, and many others. Can be expensive.
Public Transport:

Information: 0161-228-7811
Station: Old Trafford Metro Link
Buses: 252, 253, 254, 255, 256, 257 & 263 from Piccadilly bus station.

General facilities: Executive restaurant and suites.

Tourist Information:
Manchester Visitor Centre, Town Hall extension, Lloyd Street, M60 2LA
Tel: 0161-436 3344
Fax: 0161-236-9900

Directions by road:
From north, west or east: M62 to junction 12, M602 to end of motorway, at roundabout turn right, take A5063 Trafford Road. Turn right into A56 Chester Road and ground is on right. *Alternative:* M63 junction 7 take A56 towards Manchester, and park before you reach the stadium.
From south: M6 to junction 19, take A556, then A56. Pass M63 junction, and park before you reach the stadium. *Alternative:* M6 to junction 22, then M62 east, then as above. This may be very busy on match days.
N.B. Do not confuse with the Lancashire Cricket ground, which is nearby, and also called Old Trafford.

Local map: See page 92

The Vetch Field, Swansea City FC

Description of ground: One modern stand behind goal. Main stand on one side, rest of ground covered terracing. Very close to city centre.

Ground address: Vetch Field, Swansea, SA1 3SU
Ground telephone No.: 01792-474 114
Capacity: 16,355
Number of seats: 3,352

Disabled supporters:
Facilities:
Wheelchair access: Room for 12
Disabled toilets: No
The Blind: No special facilities

Food and drink: Snack bars in ground.

Transport:
Car parking: Free car parking at County Hall. Also street parking.
Public Transport:

Nearest BR station: Swansea (15-20 minutes walk from ground)
Buses: Bus stop HC at station: buses 1, 1A & 2. Quadrant bus station 100 yards from ground.

Tourist Information:
Swansea Tourist Information Centre, P.O. Box 59, Singleton St, Swansea SA1 3QG
Tel: 01792-468321

Directions by road:

From east: M4, take junction 42 onto A483 into Swansea. Stay on A483 into city centre, then take A4067, which becomes Oystermouth Road. Turn left to County Hall car park. From there walk to ground, down Paxton Street, and ground is on left behind prison. Parking is very restricted around ground on match days.

Local map: See page 92

Wembley Stadium

Description of ground: 80,000 all seated stadium. Views from lower tiers can be poor, especially in a large crowd.

Ground address: Wembley Way, Middlesex HA9 ODW
Ground telephone No.: 0181-902 8833
Capacity: 80,000
Number of seats: 80,000
Advance ticket availability: Yes

Disabled supporters:
Wheelchair access: 40 places
Disabled toilets: Yes
The Blind: No special facilities

Food and drink:
Plenty of snack bars.

Transport:
Car parking: 7,000 vehicles. It can be easier to park at a station and travel to Wembley by train.
Public transport: Information: 0171-222-1234
Nearest Underground Station: Wembley Park (Metropolitan & Jubilee lines)
Nearest BR station: Wembley Central and Wembley Stadium
Buses: 18, 83, 92, 182 & 192.

General facilities:
Restaurant, banqueting hall, stadium tours (not on match days).

Tourist Information:
London Tourist Board, 26, Grosvenor Gardens, SW1W 01DU
Telephone:
0171-824-8844 (accommodation) or 0839-123456.

Directions by road:
From north: M1 or A1 to North Circular Road (A406), head west, and take A4088, signposted Wembley. Alternative: stay on North Circular, and take A404, Harrow Road, also signposted.
N.B. Two possible alternatives. Park in Regents Park, walk to Baker Street station, and take Metropolitan line to Wembley Park. Or, park at Stanmore station, and take Jubilee line to Wembley Park. However, this car park can become full for a major match, and street parking is restricted in the area.
Local map: See page 93

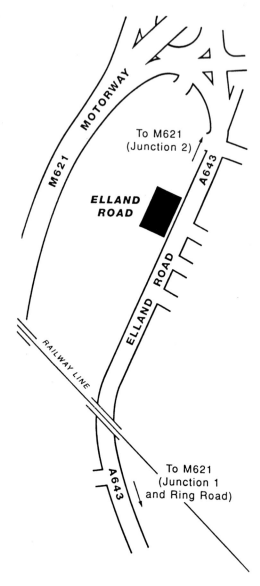

Elland Road

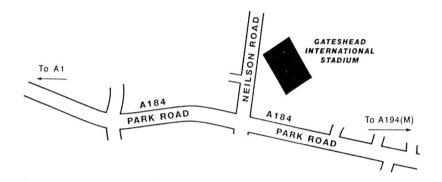

Gateshead International Stadium

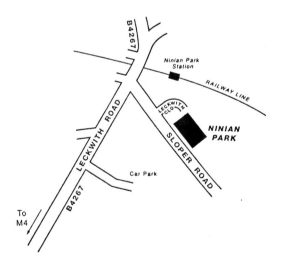

Ninian Park

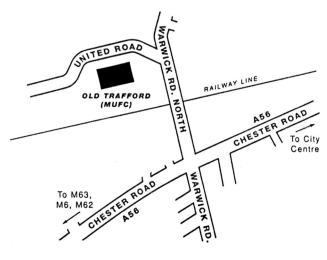

Old Trafford

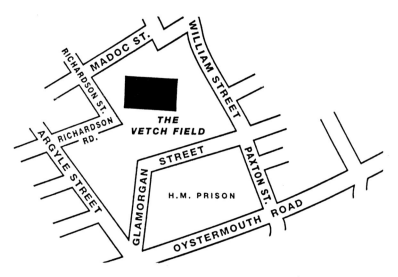

The Vetch Field

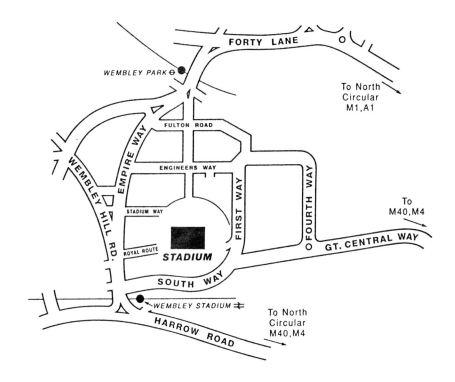

Wembley

93

BARLA National Conference Clubs

Askam
Ground Address: Fallowfield Park
Ground Tel: 01229-63320

Barrow Island
Ground Address: Rating Lane
Ground Tel: 01229-430369

Beverley
Ground Address: Beverley Town Cricket & Recreation Club, Recreation Lane, Norwood, Beverley
Ground Tel: 01482-862520

Blackbrook
Ground Address: Boardman's Lane, St Helens
Ground Tel: 01744-730492

Dewsbury Celtic
Ground Address: Crow Nest Park,Westtown, Dewsbury
Ground Tel: 01924-462615

Dudley Hill
Ground address: Neil Hunt Memorial Ground, Parry Lane, Bradford BD5
Ground Tel: 01274-669276

East Leeds
*Ground address:*Richmond Hill, 81 Easy Road, Leeds 9
Ground Tel: O113-2480101

Eastmoor
*Ground address:*King George V Playing Fields, Woodhouse Road, Eastmoor, Wakefield
Ground Tel: 01924-375367

Eccles
*Ground address:*Hallsworth Road, Off Schofield Road, Eccles
Ground Tel: 0161-788-0011

Egremont Rangers
*Ground address:*Gillfoot Park, Egremont, Cumbria
Ground Tel: 01946-820798

Hemel Hempstead
*Ground address:*Pennine Way, Hemel Hempstead HP2
Ground Tel: 01442-252258

Heworth
*Ground address:*The Clubhouse, Elm Park Way, York Y02
Ground Tel: 01904-421075

Hull Dockers
Ground address: Tower Grange, Willows, Southcotes Avenue, Hull
Ground Tel: 01482-376404

Leigh East
Ground address: Grasmere Street, Leigh, Lancs
Ground Tel: 01942-608704

Leigh Miners Welfare
Ground address: Twist Lane, Leigh, Lancs
Ground Tel: 01942-672984

Lock Lane
Ground address: The Early Bath, Wheldon Road, Castleford
Ground Tel: 01977-518389

Mayfield
Ground address: Keswick Street, Castleton, Rochdale
Ground Tel: 01706-527160

Milford
Ground address: Beckett Park, Queenswood Drive, Leeds
Ground Tel: 0113-278-3087

Millom
Ground address: Coronation Field, Devonshire Road, Millom, Cumbria
Ground Tel: 01229-772030

Moldgreen
Ground address: Ridgeway Playing Fields, Dalton
Ground Tel: 01484-516441

New Earswick All Blacks
Ground address: New Earswick Sports Ground, White Rose Ave, York
Ground Tel: 01904-750103

Normanton
Ground address: Queen Elizabeth Drive, Normanton
Ground Tel: 01924-897081

Oldham St. Annes
Ground address: Higginshaw Road, Oldham
Ground Tel: 0161-678-8660

Oulton
Ground address: Rothwell Sports Centre Ground, Oulton Green, Woodlesford, Leeds 26
Ground Tel: 0113-282-2356

Ovenden
Ground address: Four Fields, Ovenden, Halifax
Ground Tel: 01422-347739

Redhill
Ground address: Carlyle Road, Airedale, Castleford
Ground Tel: 01977-512958

Saddleworth Rangers
Ground address: Shawhall Bank Road, Greenfield, Oldham
Ground Tel: 01457-876077

Shaw Cross
Ground address: Leeds Road, Shaw Cross, Dewsbury
Ground Tel: 01924-463987

Thornhill
Ground address: Overthorpe Park,
Thornhill, Dewsbury
Ground Tel: 01924-464164

Walney Central
Ground address: Central Park,
Central Drive, Barrow-in-Furness
Secretary Tel: 01229-471926

West Hull
Ground address: The Circle,
Anlaby Road, Hull
Secretary Tel: 01482-504109

Wigan St. Judes
Ground address: Parsons Meadow,
Keats Avenue, Poolstock
Ground Tel: 01942-826808

Wigan St. Patricks
Ground address: Clarington Park,
Harper St, Wigan
Ground Tel: 01942-495071

Woolston Rovers
Ground address: Bennett's
Recreation Ground, Padgate,
Warrington
Ground Tel: 01925-812007

York Acorn
Ground address: Acorn Sports &
Social Club, Thanet Road, York
Secretary Tel: 01904-659517

For further information about amateur matches, contact:

BARLA
West Yorkshire House
4, New North Parade
Huddersfield HD1 5JP

Tel: 01484-544131
Fax: 01484-519985

We recommend checking in the press or with the home club before travelling
to any amateur matches, to check venue, kick off time etc.

London Amateur Rugby League

Aylesbury Bears
Secretary: 01296-87399

Ashford
Secretary: 01233-621600

Basingstoke Beasts
Secretary: 01256-467965

Bexleyheath*
Secretary: 01689-859178

Bognor Regis*
Secretary: 01243-841177

Brent Ealing
Secretary: 0181-723-9719

Cambridge Eagles
Secretary: 01223-414016

East London
Secretary: 0181-517-2778

Fulham Travellers
Secretary: 01932-781917

Hemel Hempstead
Ground: 01442-219799

Huntingdon Bombers:
Secretary: 01480-494723

Ipswich
Secretary: 01394-671140

London Colonials
Secretary: 0181-241-5712

London Warriors
Secretary: 0171-244-7866
(SANZ Shipping)

Metropolitan Police
Secretary: 0181-204-7974

Peckham
Secretary: 0181-677-5160

Peterborough*
Secretary: 01778-343858

Reading
Secretary: 01734-613981

Student Rugby League Old Boys
Secretary: 0181-361-6911

Surrey Heath
Secretary: 01344-488521

Swindon Bulldogs
Secretary: 01993-843363

United Services
Secretary: 01634-402025

Uxbridge Blues
Secretary: 01895-810504

* Not playing in 1995/6 season .

London clubs have a high turnover of contact numbers. For the latest information about London Amateur Rugby League telephone the Secretary, Henry Miles, on 0181-743-3455. *Time Out* usually provides information about matches.

South Wales

South Wales are playing 6 matches at Aberavon RUFC, and 6 matches at a stadium in Cardiff or Newport, not decided at the time of writing. Details below relate to Aberavon RUFC's Talbot Athletic Ground. Check with press for venue of games.

Description of ground: Main grandstand on one side. Covered terrace behind one goal.
Ground address: Talbot Athletic Ground, Manor Street, Port Talbot, Glamorgan.
Ground telephone number: 01639-886038
Office telephone number: 01222-641111 (Mike Nicholas)
Food and drink: Two bars
Transport:
Nearest BR station: Port Talbot
Tourist Information:
Llandovery office: 01792-813030. Port Talbot Council: 01639-875311
There is more hotel accommodation in the Swansea area: Swansea Tourist Information: 01792-468321.

Directions by road: M6 south, take junction 8 M5 south. Junction 8 take M50 towards South Wales. At end of motoroway, take A40, then A449 towards Newport. Join M4 at junction 24 and take M4 west to junction 40, singposted Port Talbot A4107. At roundabout, turn left into Abbey Road, and immediately right into Tan-Y-Groes Street. Turn right into Dan-Y-Bryn and Manor Street is first left.

(N.B. Unlike other grounds, we have not been able to visit Aberavon RUFC to check the above directions, as the Club's inclusion in the League was only announced five days before we went to press.)

Useful Information

Rugby League organisations:

The Rugby Football League
Red Hall House
Red Hall Lane
Leeds LS17 8NB
Telephone: 0113-232-9111or 0113-232-9444 (Box office)

The British Amateur Rugby League Association
West Yorkshire House
4, New North Parade
Huddersfield HD1 5JP
Telephone: 01484-544131
Fax: 01484-519985

Rugby League Supporters organisations:

The Rugby League Supporters Association
Membership:
5, Peregrine Crescent
Droylsden,
Manchester M43 7TA

General enquiries:
5, Wesley Street
Cutsyke
Castleford WF10 5HQ

Yorkshire Federation of Supporters Clubs
Neil Smith
57, King George Square
Kirk Sandall
Doncaster DN3 1PQ
Telephone: 01302-883771

Lancashire Federation of Supporters Clubs
Alice Collinge
95, Wimbledon Road
Failsworth
Oldham M35
Telephone: 0161-633-6780

Travel information

AA Roadwatch - Latest Traffic News

0336 401 plus the area number you require - as listed below

National motorways	110	London and South East:	
West Country	111	Area within M25	122
Wales	112	Essex, Herts, Beds,	
Midlands	113	Bucks, Oxon, Berks	123
East Anglia	114	Hants, Surrey,	
NW England	115	Sussex, Kent	125
NE England	116	M25 and link roads	127
Scotland	117		

(Calls are charged at 39p per minute cheap rate, 49p per minute at all other times)

Highways Agency

Motorway roadworks hotline: 0345-504030
Motorway roadworks information (Yorkshire & Humberside): 0345-622622

Teletext:

BBC Ceefax: Page 501-507
Teletext UK: Page 191-193

Local Radio

Local radio stations are a good source of travel information. The BBC stations in the North also cover games and give information if games are on in bad weather.

All frequencies are FM, except where indicated.

BBC Radio Cumbria	96.1 and 95.6 (and 756, 837 & 1458 AM)
BBC Radio Humberside	95.9 (and 1485 AM)
BBC Radio Lancashire	95.5, 103.9 & 104.5 (and 855 & 1557 AM)
BBC Radio Leeds	103.9 (and 774 AM)
BBC Radio London	94.9
BBC Radio Manchester (GMR)	95.1
BBC Radio Merseyside	95.8 (and 1485 AM)
BBC Radio Newcastle	95.4, (and 1458 AM)
BBC Radio Sheffield	88.6 (and 855 & 1035 AM)
BBC Radio York	95.5 (and 666 AM)
BBC Radio Wales	882 AM

The Rugby League press:

League Express:	01274-391518
Open Rugby:	0113-245-1560
Rugby Leaguer:	01942-228000
The Greatest Game:	via Rugby League Supporters Association

Notes

Add your own information - local pubs, improvements to our routes etc!

Advertisements

Support these organisations that support Rugby League and London League Publications Ltd.:

City Financial Partners Ltd
Friends of London Rugby League
League Express
Lloyds Bank
London Broncos Supporters Club
London Calling! fanzine
MH Publications
Open Rugby
Rugby League Supporters Association
Rugby Leaguer
Sportspages
Touch and Go - London League Publications

Financial Advice

FOR RUGBY FANS
(AND READERS OF BOOKS.........)

CONTACT CHRIS McCRACKEN
FOR A CONFIDENTIAL
WEALTH CHECK.

CITY FINANCIAL PARTNERS LIMITED
REPRESENTING
LINCOLN
NATIONAL
Russell Square House
10-12 Russell Square
LONDON
WC1B 5EH
Tel.: 0171-323-2828

FRIENDS OF LONDON RUGBY LEAGUE

Background history: The *Friends* were founded in 1986 with the aim of keeping professional Rugby League alive in the capital. This we helped to achieve and between 1986 and 1994 we raised well over £100,000 for this purpose.

Broncos: The advent of the London Broncos in March 1994 with the backing of the successful Brisbane Club has hopefully put the professional team on a sound financial basis and allowed the independent *Friends* to broaden their support for Rugby League in the south.

Current objectives: We now have a two-fold programme of financial assistance.

Firstly: We will continue to support the Broncos and have chosen to adopt the Alliance and future youth teams as a particular avenue for spending.

Secondly: We can provide help for the amateur game. One of the Broncos' avowed intentions is to develop Rugby League at grassroots level and to this end the *Friends* Committee are open to requests for financial aid from amateur, student, school or youth projects.

The following amateur clubs have received financial help in the last two years:

Aylesbury Bears	*Brent-Ealing*	*Peckham*
Ashford (Romney)	*Cambridge Eagles*	*Student Old Boys*
Basingstoke Beasts	*East London*	*Surrey Heath*
Bexleyheath	*Ipswich Rhinos*	*Uxbridge Blues*

The money has been used for playing strips, posts, Puma Little League Kits, school schemes, cups and balls. Larger ventures such as the acquisition of a mini-bus and the setting up of a Sports Injury Clinic have also received help.

For further details and membership application forms please apply to the Secretary:
Henry Miles
29, Mark Mansions, Westville Road, Shepherds Bush, London W12 9PS.
Telephone: 0181-743-3455 (answering machine available)

we've got it covered

Your local supporter.

We wish you every success
and are delighted to offer our
support to your organisation.

32 Oxford Street,

London W1A 2LD.

Telephone (0171) 636 8696.

London Broncos Rugby League
Supporters Club

ARE YOU BRONCO MAD?
DO YOU WANT TO KNOW MORE?
THEN JOIN THE SUPPORTERS CLUB!!!

Do you:

* Want to follow the club home and away?
* Want to discuss club matters with the people who matter?
* Socialise with fellow fans, players and club officials?

Then Join the Broncos Supporters Club!!!

Membership entitles you to attend regular meetings, have the benefit of subsidised travel as well as concessions from the club shop plus priority on tickets for all social events

The Supporters Club is a democratic body and holds elections for all positions at the AGM. We also keep in touch with other supporters throughout the country via our membership of the Lancashire and Yorkshire Supporters Federations and the Rugby League Supporters Association.

To join the London Broncos Rugby League Supporters Club and for further details / application form, please ring 01322-528504 or call into the Club Shop on matchdays.

LONDON CALLING!

The Independent London Broncos Rugby League fanzine

Established May 1993

Britain's premier Rugby League fanzine is proud to be involved again in London League Publications' new title.

Read us every month of the season for:

*   Home and away Broncos match reports
*   Local amateur Rugby League news
*   Our own Fantasy Rugby League competition
*   Being an Independent voice
*   Damn good value - still only £1
*   Not being the matchday programme

Produced independently for and by fans, *London Calling!* is on sale at the Valley on home match days, in the Club Shop, at *Sportspages* branches in London & Manchester, and also by subscription.

Copy and letters to:

Subscriptions and back issues:

London Calling! Fanzine
45, Estella Avenue
New Malden
Surrey KT3 6HX

London League Publications Ltd
P.O. Box 10441
London E14 0SB

Subscriptions:
£3 for 4 issues - special introductory offer
£7 for 8 issues
£15 for 16 issues
Back issues £1 each with A4 SAE.
Cheques payable to *London Calling!* Fanzine

Who's Fast ? Well if you really want to know, read:

Ray Hewson's

They
Could Catch
Pigeons

A History Of Speed In The Game Of Rugby League
(Foreword by Robert Gate ,Rugby League's Official Historian.)

The book will enthrall serious followers of the greatest game. Journey from Fiji to Fartown, from the Stawell Gift Sprint Championship in Australia to the Olympic Games and from Dally Messenger to Martin Offiah.

The Author has a profound knowledge of Sprinting and The Fast Men who have played League world wide. He is eminently suitable to provide this work which should become standard R.L. literature.

Extract from Foreword by Official Rugby League Historian, Robert Gate:-
"Ray Hewson is a braver man than I am. He must be - otherwise he would never have attempted to write a book like *They Could Catch Pigeons*.
His self-imposed task of defining the fastest men to have played Rugby League could only be a journey through a sporting mine-field. Everywhere he trod was liable to blow up in his face. He was certainly never likely to please everyone and that is possibly why *They Could Catch Pigeons* is such a provocative and absorbing exercise."

**ORDER THIS NEW,EXCITING PAPERBACK
ONLY £6.50 inc. p. & p. CASH/POSTAL ORDER/CHEQUE TO:
D.M.WEIR, c/o 2, Cumbria View, Walney Island, Barrow-in-
Furness, Cumbria LA14 3HP.
Published By** MH Publications

YOU LIKE RUGBY LEAGUE?

YOU'LL *LOVE* "OPEN RUGBY"!

No Rugby League fan, or anybody who appreciates high-quality
sports magazines, should miss **"OPEN RUGBY"**.

The monthly League magazine brings you in-depth articles, features
and informed comment from around the Rugby League world.
PLUS, the most sparkling colour photographs you'll ever see.

"OPEN RUGBY" is the perfect magazine for Rugby League fans -
in glorious full colour. Order your copy now !

Available by mail order

Send NOW for your sample copy: price £2.40 (inc. postage).

Or guarantee your copy for the next 12 issues by booking
a postal subscription: price £29.00

International prices:
Europe £36, Zone 1 (airmail) £47,
Zone 2 (airmail) £49, surface mail £34.

And every month **"OPEN RUGBY"** will be delivered through
your letterbox.

CREDIT CARD ORDER BY PHONE

(or call us if you want to know more about "OPEN RUGBY")

0113 - 2451560 or order by Fax: 0113-242-6255

OPEN RUGBY, Munro House, York Street, Leeds LS9 8AP.

'EYUP OLD COCK!

HAVE YOU EVER FELT FRUSTRATED BECAUSE YOU DON'T FEEL REPRESENTED AS A SUPPORTER OF RUGBY LEAGUE?

DO YOU HAVE A POINT YOU'D LIKE TO MAKE, BUT DON'T FEEL THAT THERE'S ANYWHERE FOR YOU TO MAKE IT?

DO YOU WANT TO BE CONSULTED ABOUT THE WAY THE SUPER LEAGUE IS STRUCTURED AND RUN?

ARE YOU TIRED OF BEING LABELLED A FLATCAPPED WHIPPET FANCIER BY THE PRESS, JUST BECAUSE YOU LIKE RUGBY LEAGUE?

DO YOU WANT TO RECEIVE TGG!, THE WORLDS BEST RUGBY LEAGUE FANZINE, BEFORE ANYONE ELSE?

MAYBE YOU DO.

SO MAYBE YOU OUGHT TO JOIN THE R.L.S.A. NOW, AND BECOME PART OF THE ONLY NATIONAL RL SUPPORTERS ASSOCIATION IN THE U.K.

M.A.Wilde, 1995

OUR AGENDA :

- **to democratically represent the views of members**
- **to campaign for supporters' opinions to be heard at all levels in the game**
- **to encourage friendship between supporters of all clubs and countries**
- **to work for the promotion and development of Rugby League, the greatest game of all.**

For more information please write to :

THE RUGBY LEAGUE SUPPORTERS' ASSOCIATION
5 WESLEY STREET
CUTSYKE
CASTLEFORD
WEST YORKSHIRE : WF10 5HQ

Six years experience of working for supporters!

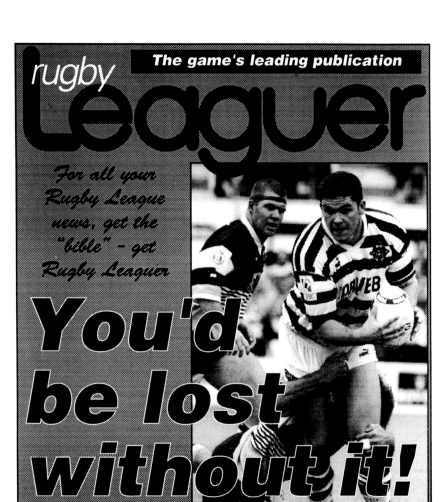

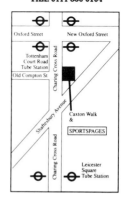

Also published by London League Publications Ltd:

Touch and Go

A History of Professional Rugby League in London

The first book about professional Rugby League in London

Features include:

* The clubs of 1930s: London Highfield, Acton & Willesden and Streatham & Mitcham
* The full histories of Fulham, the London Crusaders and London Broncos
* Coverage of internationals in the capital & the first Wembley Cup Final
* . With full statistics, interviews and pen pictures of all the key players.
* 380 pages and over 70 photographs

" A Superb New Book" - Review in the *Rugby Leaguer*

**"Tremendously good value for money... The scope of "Touch and Go" is almost breathtaking....this excellent book"
Review by Robert Gate in *League Express***

Special offer for readers of this book:

A copy of Touch and Go for £9.00 - post free.

Order from:

London League Publications,
P.O. Box 10441
London E14 OSB.

Please make cheques payable to "London League Publications Ltd"